The impact of the railways in the East End 1835–2010

Historical archaeology from the London Overground East London line

MOLA Monograph Series

For more information about these titles and other MOLA publications
visit the publications page at www.museumoflondonarchaeology.org.uk

1 Excavations at the priory and hospital of St Mary Spital, London

2 The National Roman Fabric Reference Collection: a handbook

3 The Cross Bones burial ground, Redcross Way, Southwark, London:
archaeological excavations (1991–8) for the London Underground Limited Jubilee
Line Extension Project

4 The eastern cemetery of Roman London: excavations 1983–90

5 The Holocene evolution of the London Thames: archaeological excavations
(1991–8) for the London Underground Limited Jubilee Line Extension Project

6 The Limehouse porcelain manufactory: excavations at 108–116 Narrow Street,
London, 1990

7 Roman defences and medieval industry: excavations at Baltic House, City of
London

8 London bridge: 2000 years of a river crossing

9 Roman and medieval townhouses on the London waterfront: excavations at
Governor's House, City of London

10 The London Charterhouse

11 Medieval 'Westminster' floor tiles

12 Settlement in Roman Southwark: archaeological excavations (1991–8) for the
London Underground Limited Jubilee Line Extension Project

13 Aspects of medieval and later Southwark: archaeological excavations (1991–8)
for the London Underground Limited Jubilee Line Extension Project

14 The prehistory and topography of Southwark and Lambeth

15 Middle Saxon London: excavations at the Royal Opera House 1989–99

16 Urban development in north-west Roman Southwark: excavations 1974–90

17 Industry in north-west Roman Southwark: excavations 1984–8

18 The Cistercian abbey of St Mary Stratford Langthorne, Essex: archaeological
excavations for the London Underground Limited Jubilee Line Extension Project

19 Material culture in London in an age of transition: Tudor and Stuart period finds
c 1450–c 1700 from excavations at riverside sites in Southwark

20 Excavations at the priory of the Order of the Hospital of St John of Jerusalem,
Clerkenwell, London

21 Roman and medieval Cripplegate, City of London: archaeological excavations
1992–8

22 The royal palace, abbey and town of Westminster on Thorney Island:
archaeological excavations (1991–8) for the London Underground Limited Jubilee
Line Extension Project

23 A prestigious Roman building complex on the Southwark waterfront: excavations
at Winchester Palace, London, 1983–90

24 Holy Trinity Priory, Aldgate, City of London: an archaeological reconstruction
and history

25 Roman pottery production in the Walbrook valley: excavations at 20–28
Moorgate, City of London, 1998–2000

26 Prehistoric landscape to Roman villa: excavations at Beddington, Surrey, 1981–7

27 Saxon, medieval and post-medieval settlement at Sol Central, Marefair,
Northampton: archaeological excavations, 1998–2002

28 John Baker's late 17th-century glasshouse at Vauxhall

29 The medieval postern gate by the Tower of London

30 Roman and later development east of the forum and Cornhill: excavations at
Lloyd's Register, 71 Fenchurch Street, City of London

31 Winchester Palace: excavations at the Southwark residence of the bishops of
Winchester

32 Development on Roman London's western hill: excavations at Paternoster Square,
City of London

33 Within these walls: Roman and medieval defences north of Newgate at the
Merrill Lynch Financial Centre, City of London

34 The Augustinian priory of St Mary Merton, Surrey: excavations 1976–90

35 London's Roman amphitheatre: excavations at the Guildhall

36 The London Guildhall: an archaeological history of a neighbourhood from early
medieval to modern times

37 Roman London and the Walbrook stream crossing: excavations at 1 Poultry and
vicinity, City of London

38 The development of early medieval and later Poultry and Cheapside: excavations
at 1 Poultry and vicinity, City of London

39 Burial at the site of the parish church of St Benet Sherehog before and after the
Great Fire: excavations at 1 Poultry, City of London

40 London's delftware industry: the tin-glazed pottery industries of Southwark and
Lambeth

41 Early and Middle Saxon rural settlement in the London region

42 Roman Southwark settlement and economy: excavations in Southwark 1973–91

43 The Black Death cemetery, East Smithfield, London

44 The Cistercian abbey of St Mary Graces, East Smithfield, London

45 The Royal Navy victualling yard, East Smithfield, London

46 St Marylebone Church and burial ground in the 18th to 19th centuries:
excavations at St Marylebone School, 1992 and 2004–6

47 Great houses, moats and mills on the south bank of the Thames: medieval and
Tudor Southwark and Rotherhithe

48 The Rose and the Globe – playhouses of Shakespeare's Bankside, Southwark:
excavations 1988–91

49 A dated type series of London medieval pottery: Part 5, Shelly-sandy ware and
the greyware industries

50 The Cluniac priory and abbey of St Saviour Bermondsey, Surrey: excavations
1984–95

51 Three Ways Wharf, Uxbridge: a Lateglacial and Early Holocene hunter-gatherer
site in the Colne valley

52 The impact of the railways in the East End 1835–2010: historical archaeology from
the London Overground East London line

The impact of the railways in the East End 1835–2010

Historical archaeology from the London Overground East London line

Emma Dwyer

MOLA MONOGRAPH 52

MUSEUM OF LONDON ARCHAEOLOGY

Published by Museum of London Archaeology
Copyright © Museum of London 2011

A CIP catalogue record for this book is available from the British Library

Production and series design by Tracy Wellman
Typesetting and design by Sue Cawood
Reprographics by Andy Chopping
Copy editing by Simon Burnell
Series editing by Sue Hirst/Susan M Wright

Printed by the Lavenham Press

Front cover: Over London by rail *by Gustave Doré, 1872 (Museum of
London, LIB5788)*

CONTRIBUTORS

Principal author	Emma Dwyer
Additional material	Nigel Jeffries
Documentary research	Christopher Phillpotts with Emma Dwyer, Rupert Featherby
Clay tobacco pipes	Tony Grey
Pottery	Lyn Blackmore (site C), Nigel Jeffries (site F), Jacqui Pearce (site B)
Accessioned finds	Geoff Egan (site B), Beth Richardson (site C)
Glass	Lyn Blackmore, Geoff Egan (site F)
Graphics	Valeria Boesso, Mark Burch, Catherine Drew, Carlos Lemos
Studio photography	Andy Chopping
Site photography	Maggie Cox, David Mansell
Project managers	George Dennis, Elaine Eastbury, Nicholas Elsden, Nicola Powell
Editor	Helen Dawson

CONTENTS

Introduction   **1**

The development of the railways   **2**

Shoreditch below ground: archaeological evidence for clearance, and the construction of the Eastern Counties Railway   **3**

FIGURES

TABLES

SUMMARY

The upgrade and extension of the East London line of the London Underground as part of London Overground provided an opportunity to examine life in London's inner city and suburban districts between the 19th and 21st centuries, and the impact that the construction and development of the railways had on life for Londoners. An extensive programme of built heritage recording was carried out, from Dalston in the north to Surrey Quays in the south, and in this volume is integrated with the data from excavations at the site of Bishopsgate goods station and Lee Street in Haggerston, shedding light on life in these areas before the arrival of the railways, and the resulting tumult for the occupants of the East End.

The Eastern Counties Railway, which opened in 1840, was one of London's earliest railways and, unlike its contemporaries the Great Western Railway and the London and Birmingham Railway, cut through the crowded streets and industries of the East End; the results from excavations at Bishopsgate goods station provide an insight into life in the inner-city districts of Shoreditch and Spitalfields immediately before and during the construction of the railway. Consideration is given to the role that railways and their associated structures, which were entirely new kinds of buildings in the mid 19th century, played in shaping the lives of East Enders, how they moved around the city and how they regarded their neighbours.

While the Eastern Counties Railway was part of a first wave of railway building in Britain, spanning the country, transporting goods and people over long distances, and inspiring breathless, awe-struck accounts of train travel by travel writers, the excitement was short-lived. Twenty years later the construction of local railways, like the North London Railway and the East London Railway, linked the disparate communities and industries of urban centres like London, facilitating urban sprawl and allowing the creation of the metropolis. The East London Railway had its roots in the Thames Tunnel, designed and built by Sir Marc Brunel with the assistance of his son Isambard Kingdom Brunel. The tunnel was intended to connect communities and industries on both sides of the Thames, but was an economic failure; construction of the tunnel began in 1825 and continued intermittently for 18 years. The East London Railway Company bought the tunnel and converted it to form part of its new railway, which later became the East London line of the London Underground. From the 1860s the North London Railway transformed Dalston from an outlying village to a thriving inner-city district, bursting with pubs, cinemas and restaurants, which were countered by the alcohol-free entertainment offered for example by the Tee-To-Tum Tea Stores in Kingsland High Street.

Archaeological studies of the built environment have traditionally focused on buildings being 'read' and understood as they were intended to be by those responsible for their construction. This publication aims to go beyond understanding and interpreting the intended uses of buildings and structures, acknowledging the messy biographies and multiple lives of the buildings around us by looking at both the intended uses and 'afterlife' of the historic built environment.

ACKNOWLEDGEMENTS

The programmes of archaeological excavation and built heritage recording associated with the extension of the East London line, and the subsequent analysis and publication, were funded by Transport for London (TfL); particular thanks are due to Jon Colclough of TfL and Steve Haynes of Arup for their unstinting support and enthusiasm for the project. The archaeological work and built heritage recording was monitored by David Divers of the Greater London Archaeology Advisory Service, English Heritage.

The staff of the Taylor Woodrow and then Balfour Beatty Carillion Joint Venture and of the London Underground East London line stations facilitated access to sites and gave freely of their time; the tenants of the Pedley Street railway arches, and of the shops and buildings in Dalston, were particularly patient and helpful during the building recording project.

The staff of several museums, libraries and local archives, and members of special interest societies provided valuable knowledge and assistance, namely Rabbi Dr Walter Rothschild of the London Metropolitan Archive; the National Monuments Record Centre, Swindon; Essex Records Office; Hackney Local Studies Library; Tower Hamlets Local History Library; Southwark Local History Library; the Great Eastern Railway Society; the North London Railway Society; the British Library; the National Railway Museum, York; the Brunel Museum, Rotherhithe; the Jewish Museum, London; and the London Transport Museum, in particular Robert Excell and Matthew Caro.

The excavations at Bishopsgate goods station were supervised by Aaron Birchenough and Hana Lewis, and the built heritage recording was carried out by Emma Dwyer, Andrew Westman, Patrizia Pierazzo, David Sorapure, Al Telfer, Paul Thrale and Mark Wiggins. The digital survey of the Pedley Street and Grimsby Street viaducts and Bishopsgate goods station was carried out by Eamonn Baldwin, Mark Burch, Neville Constantine, Simon Davis and Catherine Drew.

Marilyn Palmer (University of Leicester) and Tony Taylor (formerly of Foggo Associates) provided ongoing academic advice and valuable technical insight, which has added a further dimension to the project.

1

Introduction

1.1 Locations and circumstances of fieldwork

This monograph provides an account of the built heritage recording undertaken along the route of the extension of the East London line of the London Underground, prior to its incorporation into the London Overground network, the capital's newest urban railway (Fig 1). Recording was undertaken at a number of sites, including the East London line's existing stations, and along the route of the line's northern and southern extensions (Table 1).

This publication also contains an account of the below-ground archaeological evidence from excavations at Bishopsgate goods station and Grimsby Street, relating to the phases of clearance, construction and occupation associated with the Great Eastern Railway viaduct and Shoreditch station, which opened in 1840, and the Bishopsgate goods station, which opened in 1882.

The Pedley Street and Grimsby Street viaduct (site A)

The construction of a ramp and portal on the northern side of Pedley Street, E2, where the East London line trains could emerge from the line's existing tunnel and then be carried over Brick Lane on a new bridge, necessitated the demolition of a section of the 1840 Braithwaite viaduct in Pedley Street and a later extension to the viaduct, constructed in the 1880s, in Grimsby Street. The demolition took place, after a programme of standing building recording, during the summer of 2007. While the viaduct in Pedley Street and Grimsby Street was not statutorily listed, to the west of the site 20 arches of the Braithwaite viaduct on the western side of Brick Lane, within the former Bishopsgate goods station, were statutorily listed as a building of special historical or architectural interest, grade II, in 2002 (Listed Buildings System (LBS) no. 488529). To the east of the site, two further stretches of the Braithwaite viaduct in Stepney (LBS nos 788/0/10160 and 788/0/10171) were statutorily listed, grade II, in September 2007. The programme of building recording began in August 2006, while the arches underneath the viaduct were still occupied and being used by various businesses, including motor garages and furniture makers.

Bishopsgate goods station (sites B and C)

Bishopsgate goods station closed to rail traffic following a fire in December 1964, but subsequently had many uses; it became a car-breaker's yard, car park, and later a gym complex and entertainment venue, before the extension of the East London line was announced. Construction of the new elevated railway line and a station in Shoreditch High Street required the demolition of much of the former goods station, although the location of the National Rail lines into Liverpool Street station on the southern side of the site meant that demolition and

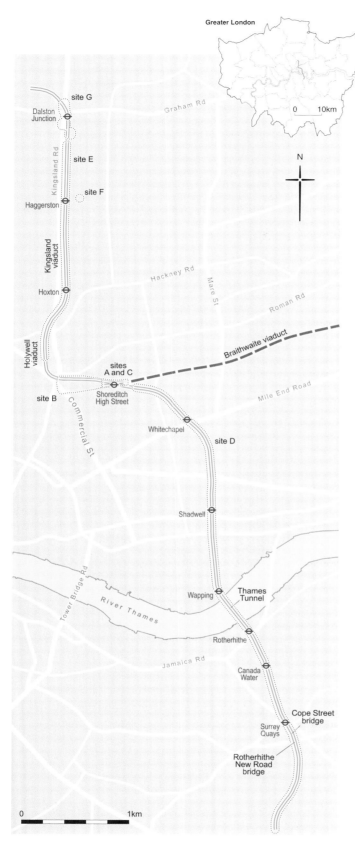

Fig 1 The locations of sites mentioned in the text (scale 1:35,000)

Table 1 Principal sites described in this report

Prefix	Site code	Address/description
A	PEL06	Braithwaite viaduct, Pedley Street, E2
B	BGX05	Bishopsgate goods station, Shoreditch High Street, E1
C	GIM07	the Great Eastern Railway viaduct, Grimsby Street, E2
D	ELE07	the stations and infrastructure of the existing East London line of the London Underground, E1–SE8 and SE16
E	KVD07	the Holywell and Kingsland viaducts of the North London Railway, EC2–E8
F	LSD05	archaeological evaluation of the rear yards of properties in Lee Street, E8
G	DJS07	historic railway infrastructure, shops and houses in the vicinity of Dalston Junction station, E8

stretch of the Braithwaite viaduct which was incorporated into the structure of the goods station has already been mentioned above, while the brick forecourt walls and wrought iron entrance gates were statutorily listed, grade II, in 1975. The building recording work was carried out at intervals between April 2003 and March 2007, as areas within the former goods station became available for survey.

The East London line of the London Underground (site D)

The East London line, which incorporates Marc Brunel's Thames Tunnel, closed in December 2007 in order to facilitate the building work required to extend the line. All of the stations, with the exception of Shoreditch underground station in Pedley Street, E2, re-opened in May 2010 as part of the London Overground network, with some minor structural and cosmetic changes. During the 1990s, London Underground carried out a heritage audit, a study of each station on the line, summarising its history and the development of the station buildings. The existing heritage audits were subsequently augmented by the results of targeted built heritage recording.

Shoreditch underground station closed permanently in June 2006, 18 months before the rest of the line. A standing building survey was carried out in advance of the station's closure, after which the station platform was dismantled and the railway cutting filled in.

The North London Railway (sites E and F)

The Holywell and Kingsland viaducts (site E) formed part of the former North London Railway (NLR), a branch of which ran from Broad Street station, on the north-eastern edge of the City of London immediately to the west of Liverpool Street

construction work was confined to the northern side of the goods station site.

The site contained two listed structures: the grade II-listed

station, to Dalston Junction, until the closure of the line in 1986. The railway line was carried north from the Broad Street terminus on three discrete viaducts, with the railway line being carried over the major thoroughfares of Great Eastern Street and Kingsland Road on bridges of riveted wrought iron plate construction. As the railway line approached the higher ground of Dalston, it entered a cutting, enabling the line to pass below the centre of the suburb.

The Holywell viaduct, which stands on the western side of Shoreditch High Street to the north of Great Eastern Street, and the Kingsland viaduct, on the eastern side of Kingsland Road, have been retained and reused for the East London line extension. A photographic survey of the viaducts was carried out, and lean-to warehouses and workshops constructed on the eastern side of the railway arches in King John Court, EC1, were recorded before their demolition.

The excavation of evaluation trenches underneath one of the railway arches of the Kingsland viaduct, in Lee Street, Haggerston (site F), shed light on the lives of those who lived in the emerging suburbs in the mid 19th century, and the abandonment of homes in advance of the construction of the railway.

Dalston Junction (site G)

Dalston had been the location of Dalston Junction station on the North London Railway (NLR), which closed in 1986. The site of the former station was to be redeveloped in order to construct a new station, and a concrete slab constructed over the railway cutting to the south of Dalston Lane would also form the base for a bus station and apartment blocks. Built heritage recording focused on the historic railway infrastructure, including remnants of the station facade in Dalston Lane, cutting walls, bridges and the covered way which carried the railway line below Kingsland High Street.

A number of standing buildings were also recorded, namely:
    5–13 Roseberry Place;
    570–572 Kingsland Road;
    2 and 2A Dalston Lane;
    10–34 Kingsland High Street.
The buildings in Roseberry Place, a terrace of houses constructed before the NLR in the 1850s, were recorded during the early stages of demolition. Nos 570–572 Kingsland Road were recorded while the ground floor and basement of the shop were still in use as a branch of Oxfam. Nos 2 and 2A Dalston Lane, a former shoe shop and estate agents respectively, were recorded after the premises had been vacated. Nos 10–34 Kingsland High Street comprised several shops and the King's Arms public house; while some of the shops and the public house had closed before the building recording could take place, others remained open until the summer of 2008, allowing the buildings to be recorded while still in use.

Post-excavation

Post-excavation work on the results of the built heritage recording and excavations started after the fieldwork on all sites had been completed in July 2008. A chapter about the preliminary results of the built heritage recording of the Braithwaite viaduct and associated structures in Pedley Street and Grimsby Street was contributed to a conference volume on future directions for the archaeological study of post-medieval Britain and Ireland (Dwyer 2009), and a 'popular book' summarising the results of the fieldwork was also published (Birchenough et al 2009).

1.2　Associated archaeological excavations

A number of trenches were excavated on the site of Bishopsgate goods station (site B) between 2005 and 2007, during and after the demolition of the northern side of the goods station, facing on to Bethnal Green Road and Sclater Street. In 2007, evaluation trenches were excavated on the southern side of the junction of Grimsby Street and Brick Lane following the demolition of the Grimsby Street viaduct (site C); the results of the excavations, in so far as they relate to the character of this area of Shoreditch immediately before and during the construction of the Eastern Counties Railway (ECR), will be discussed in Chapter 3. The archaeological evidence for life in Shoreditch in the medieval and early post-medieval periods is dealt with in a separate monograph (Birchenough et al in prep).

1.3　Organisation of this report

Following this introduction, Chapter 2 will outline the development of Britain's national and local railways from the 1830s onwards, placing the development of the Eastern Counties Railway (ECR), and the later North London Railway (NLR) and East London line of the London Underground in their regional and national context. The principal features of a railway line, station and goods yard will be outlined, allowing an understanding of the features at Bishopsgate goods station, the Pedley Street viaduct, the East London line and the NLR.

Chapter 3 provides integrated chronological narratives of the excavations at the site of Bishopsgate goods station and the Grimsby Street viaduct, with regard to the character of the area and the lives of its occupants immediately before and during the construction of the ECR. Chapter 4 similarly provides an integrated chronological account of the standing structures built for the ECR and its successor organisations (the Great Eastern Railway (GER), the London and North Eastern Railway (LNER) and British Rail) and the impact that the construction of such massive structures as John Braithwaite's viaduct and the Bishopsgate goods station had on the surrounding built environment, and on the people who lived and worked in the shadow of the railway.

Chapter 5 outlines the origins of the East London line of the London Underground in Marc Brunel's failed enterprise, the Thames Tunnel, and the subsequent development of the railway line. Chapter 6 then explores the impact that the opening of the NLR's branch line from Broad Street, in the City of London, to Dalston had on the development of the latter community.

The final chapter will bring together the various strands of discussion related to the three main groups of sites treated in the volume, and consider what the project has taught us about Shoreditch and London's railways, and how it has developed new ways of thinking about London's historic transport infrastructure and the impact it has had on London's communities, past and present. This monograph seeks to provide a broader assessment of how the three railways discussed here have altered and shaped the places they have run through and affected the people living in them, both in the past and more recently, and of how such an approach might be applied to other archaeological projects.

1.4 Graphical and textual conventions used in this report

In order for the reader to be able to locate the provenance of archaeological finds or strata, site codes have been assigned to the three excavations that are included in this monograph. Two basic units are referred to in the text: the context number and (occasionally) the group number. The context number is a unique number given to each archaeological event on the site, such as a layer, cut, fill, wall and so on. During analysis the contexts are finally aggregated into groups representing more complex features on the basis of interpretation following standard MOLA practice.

Numbered archaeological contexts are noted within square brackets and prefixed by site code identifiers (letters) as listed in Table 1; thus, for example, F[4] represents context 4 from the Lee Street site (LSD05). Buildings, open areas and discrete structures identified during the archaeological fieldwork are identified by the prefix letters B, OA and S respectively. The original numbering (found in the respective site reports, where the buildings, open areas and structures were originally discussed) has been retained in this monograph. Each of these sites has its own land-use sequence beginning at 1; therefore, in order to avoid confusion, land uses are prefixed by their particular site code identifier, thus: A:B10 referring to Building 10 at site A; B:OA45 referring to Open Area 45 at site B; and F:S12 referring to Structure 12 at site F.

Several categories of finds have been numbered for illustration and/or cataloguing within this monograph, details of which are given in Tables 2–6. To indicate clearly the finds type and catalogue reference, a prefix denoting the category appears inside angled brackets with the specific artefact number, thus:

<CP1> refers to clay pipe no. 1; for details of clay pipes see Table 2;

<G3> refers to glass object no. 3; for details of glass objects see Table 3;

<P5> refers to pottery vessel no. 5; for details of pottery objects see Table 4;

<S10> refers to accessioned small find no. 10; for details of small finds see Table 5;

<T2> refers to tile no. 2; for details of tiles see Table 6.

The publication employs standard Museum of London reference codes for ceramics; these codes were developed by MOL for recording purposes. A fabric number system is used to record building materials (tile and brick); these numbers relate to detailed fabric descriptions. Pottery is recorded using codes (alphabetic or a combination of alphabetic and numeric) for fabrics, forms and decoration. Expansions of pottery codes are given at the first mention in a text section. Detailed descriptions of the building material fabrics and complete lists of the pottery codes, their expansions and date ranges are available from the LAARC as part of the research archive and are also posted on the LAARC and MOLA pages of the MOL website: www.museumoflondonarchaeology.org.uk

Some measurements cited from documents are in pre-metric imperial units: 12 inches (in) equal 1 foot (ft); 3ft equal 1 yard; 1ft equals 0.305m; an acre equals 0.4 hectares (ha). Sums of money quoted in the text, and relating to events prior to decimalisation of the currency in the United Kingdom in 1971,

Table 2 Details of clay pipes <CP1>–<CP10> referred to in the text

Catalogue no.	Site/accession no.	Site/context no.	Land use	Description	Fig no.
<CP1>	B<683>	B[1813]	B:B14	by Bernard Leach	-
<CP2>	B<684>	B[1813]	B:B14	stamped OSBORNE LONDON	-
<CP3>	C<14>	C[1]	C:B1	by Thomas Leach	-
<CP4>	C<19>	C[1]	C:B1	by William Walker	-
<CP5>	C<25>	C[2]	C:B1	with Prince of Wales feather	-
<CP6>	B<401>	B[682]	B:B39	masonic type AO30 with claw	32
<CP7>	F<1>	F[8]	-	London type with leaves	-
<CP8>	F<2>	F[8]	-	London type with ribbing	-
<CP9>	F<3>	F[8]	-	marked with WW	-
<CP10>	F<4>	F[8]	-	marked with WD	-

Table 3 Details of glass objects <G1>–<G7> referred to in the text

Catalogue no.	Site/accession no.	Site/context no.	Land use	Description	Fig no.
<G1>	C<32>	C[1]	C:B1	glass lid (with <G2>)	-
<G2>	C<33>	C[1]	C:B1	glass lid (with <G1>)	-
<G3>	C<34>	C[1]	C:B1	glass dish	-
<G4>	-	F[8]	-	oval-shaped spirit flask	113
<G5>	-	F[8]	-	sub-octagonal spirit flask	113
<G6>	-	F[8]	-	aqua medicine bottle	113
<G7>	-	F[8]	-	aqua medicine bottle	113

Table 4 Details of pottery objects <P1>–<P33> referred to in the text

Catalogue no.	Site/accession no.	Site/context no.	Land use	Fabric code	Description	Fig no.
<P1>	-	B[2057]	B:OA66	TPW3	refined whiteware pot lid with black transfer-printed decoration	9
<P2>	-	B[738]	B:B37	ENGS	English stoneware blacking paste pot	10
<P3>	-	B[171]	B:OA69	YELL	plain yellow ware deep-flared bowl	11
<P4>	-	B[171]	B:OA69	YELL SLIP	yellow ware pitcher with industrial slip decoration	11
<P5>	-	B[171]	B:OA69	NOTS	Nottingham stoneware cup	11
<P6>	-	B[171]	B:OA69	PEAR BW	pearlware saucer with underglaze blue-painted decoration	11
<P7>	-	B[171]	B:OA69	PEAR TR2	pearlware saucer with blue transfer-printed (stipple and line) decoration	11
<P8>	-	B[171]	B:OA69	PEAR TR2	pearlware rounded or slop bowl with blue transfer-printed (stipple and line) decoration	11
<P9>	-	B[171]	B:OA69	PEAR SLIP	pearlware rounded or slop bowl with industrial slip decoration	11
<P10>	-	B[171]	B:OA69	PEAR SLIP	pearlware barrel-shaped jug with industrial slip decoration	11
<P11>	-	B[171]	B:OA69	REFW	plain refined whiteware chamber pot	11
<P12>	-	B[1266]	B:B7	RBORB	Surrey-Hampshire border redware bedpan with brown glaze	18
<P13>	-	B[1266]	B:B7	RBORB	Surrey-Hampshire border redware double carinated condiment dish with brown glaze	18
<P14>	-	B[1266]	B:B7	CREA PNTD	creamware cream or milk jug with polychrome painted decoration	18
<P15>	-	B[1266]	B:B7	PEAR SLIP	pearlware salt cellar with industrial slip decoration	18
<P16>	-	B[1266]	B:B7	ENPO WORC TR	Worcester porcelain rounded bowl with blue transfer-printed decoration	18
<P17>	-	B[1266]	B:B7	CHPO ROSE	Chinese porcelain vase with *famille rose* decoration	18
<P18>	-	B[1813]	B:B14	DUTR	Dutch red earthenware brazier	19
<P19>	-	B[1310]	B:OA79	CHPO	Far Eastern porcelain dish	23
<P20>	B<443>	B[1312]	B:OA79	PIPE	Continental pipeclay figure	25
<P21>	B<1554>	B[527]	B:OA61	PEAR PNTD	pearlware figure with underglaze polychrome painted decoration, head and feet only	-
<P22>	B<1085>	B[527]	B:OA61	PEAR PNTD	pearlware female figure with underglaze polychrome painted decoration	26
<P23>	-	B[682]	B:B39	PEAR PNTD	pearlware teacup with underglaze polychrome painted decoration	32
<P24>	-	B[682]	B:B39	PEAR PNTD	pearlware saucer with underglaze polychrome painted decoration	32
<P25>	-	B[2117]	B:B39	ENGS BRST	English stoneware miniature mug with Bristol glaze	33
<P26>	-	B[523]	B:B39	BONE	bone china toy teapot	34
<P27>	-	F[8]	-	TPW5	refined whiteware pot lid with three-colour transfer-printed decoration	112
<P28>	-	F[8]	-	REFW SLIP	refined whiteware coffee can with industrial slip decoration	112
<P29>	-	F[8]	-	TPW FLOW	transfer-printed refined whiteware cream jug with 'flow blue' decoration	112
<P30>	-	F[8]	-	TPW FLOW	transfer-printed refined whiteware mug with 'flow blue' decoration, made by Davenport	112
<P31>	-	F[8]	-	ENGS	English stoneware bottle	112
<P32>	-	F[8]	-	ENGS	English stoneware bottle	112
<P33>	-	F[8]	-	TPW2	refined whiteware children's nursery mug with blue transfer-printed (stipple and line) decoration	112

are cited in £, s and d, where 12 pence (d) made one shilling (s) and 20 shillings (or 240d) a pound (£), since modern equivalents would be misleading.

County names referred to in the text refer to historic counties. The County of London was created in 1889, incorporating what had previously been loosely defined as 'the Metropolis', the urban areas situated close to the Cities of London and Westminster, and Southwark, but actually located in the counties of Middlesex, Surrey and Kent. In 1965 the County of London was abolished, and the much larger administrative area of Greater London was created, extending eastwards across the River Lea and into the county of Essex.

In order to avoid frequent repetition of the full names of former railway companies in the text, Table 7 provides a key to their abbreviations (acronyms) as used there. A glossary at the end of the text contains some of the more specialised railway and building-related terms used here. The graphical conventions used in the plans and elevations in this report are shown in Fig 2. Scales of reproduction are given in the figure captions as appropriate.

Table 5 Details of accessioned small finds <S1>–<S25> referred to in the text

Catalogue no.	Site/ accession no.	Site/ context no.	Land use	Description	Fig no.
<S1>	B<186>	B[723]	B:OA54	incomplete bone fan rib	-
<S2>	B<180>	B[723]	B:OA54	bone whistle	-
<S3>	B<179>	B[723]	B:OA54	bone spoon	-
<S4>	B<178>	B[723]	B:OA54	bone tube	-
<S5>	B<273>	B[1266]	B:B7	bone shuttle	-
<S6>	B<321>	B[1831]	B:B15	ivory waste	-
<S7>	B<1418>	B[1310]	B:OA79	cloth offcuts	-
<S8>	B<237>	B[1310]	B:OA79	iron wire, robust; spiralled, square-sectioned	-
<S9>	B<1547>	B[1310]	B:OA79	iron bolt	-
<S10>	B<1548>	B[1310]	B:OA79	iron door handle	-
<S11>	B<745>	B[1310]	B:OA79	iron ring for lining barrels	-
<S12>	B<1394>	B[1310]	B:OA79	iron sheet lining	-
<S13>	B<276>	B[1310]	B:OA79	composite wooden handle, scale-tang (half-length); drilled-hole motifs	-
<S14>	B<1087>	B[1310]	B:OA79	gun flint	-
<S15>	B<274>	B[1312]	B:OA79	bone spoon	-
<S16>	B<34>	B[512]	B:OA61	part of a bone fan	-
<S17>	B<1368>	B[512]	B:OA61	bone-working waste	-
<S18>	B<773>	B[521]	B:B28	bone-working waste	-
<S19>	B<1372>	B[548]	B:OA61	bone-working waste	-
<S20>	B<1373>	B[548]	B:OA61	bone-working waste	-
<S21>	C<42>	C[1]	C:B1	Victorian halfpenny, 1863	-
<S22>	C<40>	C[1]	C:B1	bone toothbrush	-
<S23>	C<44>	C[1]	C:B1	copper-alloy comb	-
<S24>	B<357>	B[1268]	B:OA83	bone pin or needle, head missing, abraded	31
<S25>	B<356>	B[682]	B:B39	iron bayonet	-

Table 6 Details of tiles <T1>–<T4> referred to in the text

Catalogue no.	Site/ accession no.	Site/ context no.	Land use	Description	Fig no.
<T1>	B<1446>	B[1831]	B:B51	landscape in circular border	-
<T2>	B<680>	B[617]	B:B39	with mounted soldier	35
<T3>	B<681>	B[617]	B:B39	geometric and floral pattern	35
<T4>	B<1519>	B[2117]	B:B39	medallion decoration, with hindquarters of dog	35

Table 7 Railway companies referred to in the text and the abbreviations use

ECR	Eastern Counties Railway
ELR	East London Railway
GER	Great Eastern Railway
GWR	Great Western Railway
LB&SCR	London, Brighton and South Coast Railway
LCDR	London, Chatham and Dover Railway
LMS	London, Midland and Scottish Railway
LNER	London and North Eastern Railway
LNWR	London and North Western Railway
N&ER	Northern and Eastern Railway
NLR	North London Railway
SER	South Eastern Railway
SR	Southern Railway

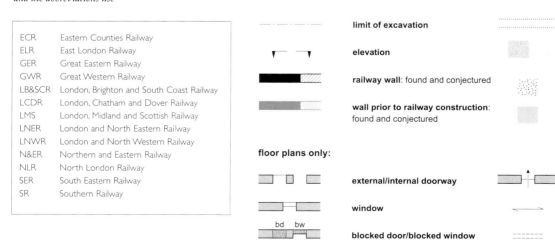

Fig 2 Graphical conventions used in this report

2

The development of the railways

The planning and construction of the Liverpool and Manchester Railway of 1830, considered to be Britain's first modern railway (in that it was formed by a public company, following an Act of Parliament, and connected the populace and industry of two metropolises), depended on technologies and legal frameworks that had been developed during the preceding 200 years.

Prototype railways had developed in Bohemia and Westphalia in central Europe in the 16th century, where they were used in mines, and were presented to the world in Georgius Agricola's *De re metallica* ('On the nature of metals') of 1556; four-wheeled wagons ran along two parallel planks, and an iron guide pin fixed to the underside of the wagon fitted in the gap between the planks, keeping the wagon from derailing (Morriss 2003, 18). The only motive power would have been provided by horses, or humans pushing the wagons by hand. During the 16th century, the mining engineers who developed such prototype railways were encouraged to settle in England and brought the technology with them. Railways and wagonways were built by individuals and companies, mainly on private land, to transport coal or stone from mines and quarries. Some of these private railways continued to be built into the 19th century, such as the complex of wagonways and sidings at Lambton colliery in Sunderland (Co Durham), where the earlier timber rails were replaced and the network was expanded to accommodate the increase in mining activity at the time (Ayris et al 1998). The development of the canal network in the 18th century led to the construction of feeder railway lines, which brought coal, stone and other materials and goods to the canal barges; transport of materials and goods over large distances was easier and cheaper by canal or river barges, or coastal shipping. In effect, these new feeder lines were open to the public, in that they could carry any kind of cargo (ibid, 21).

The methods and technologies used to build canals were easily transferred to the construction of railways, as were the legal frameworks which were necessary for large projects that required the purchase of land from a number of different parties. The world's first railway open to the public, the Surrey Iron Railway, was enabled by an Act of Parliament which was passed in 1801 (Morriss 2003, 22). The railway opened in 1803, connecting Croydon, to the south of London, with the Thames at Wandsworth; it was extended in 1805 to the chalk and lime works at Merstham, also in Surrey (Timbs 1868, 287). This railway was dedicated to the transportation of goods, and users had to pay a fee and provide their own horse and cart, making the Surrey Iron Railway more akin to the turnpike roads constructed across the country.

2.1   The early passenger railways

The introduction of steam power allowed the owners of railways to compete with the canal barges and coastal shipping, and provide a quicker and more efficient form of transport overland, making the railways more attractive as a means of transport for people rather than just goods. The early passenger railways did not depend solely on steam locomotives, however. The Stockton and Darlington Railway, which opened in 1825 and connected the town of Darlington (Co Durham) and nearby collieries with Stockton on Tees, where coal could be loaded on to sea-going boats, was powered by a combination of steam locomotives, stationary steam engines, and draught horses along different sections of the route; passenger carriages were initially hauled exclusively by horse. The Liverpool and Manchester Railway, which opened in 1830, was the first to use locomotives for both passenger and goods traffic, although stationary engines were used to bring trains into the terminus at Liverpool (Morriss 2003, 24–5).

London's first modern railway, the London and Greenwich Railway, was constructed between Greenwich and a terminus in Tooley Street, near the southern end of London Bridge, and opened in 1836. This relatively short line, 3³/₄ miles (6km) in length, would form the core of a network stretching across Kent, but for now was really a local line, competing with stagecoaches and boats on the Thames. The London and

Greenwich Railway was soon followed in 1837 by the London and Birmingham Railway, with its terminus at Euston, and the Great Western Railway, running to Paddington, in 1838 (Fig 3).

The ability to connect with other forms of transport was an important feature of the early mainline railways. The London and Birmingham line was originally intended to terminate at Chalk Farm, 1¹/₄ miles (2km) from the ultimate location of the Euston terminus, but an Act of Parliament was obtained for an extension to the Euston Road in 1835; Euston Road formed part of the New Road, a turnpike constructed during the mid 18th century to bypass the city, and became an important route in and out of the metropolis. Isambard Kingdom Brunel also carefully situated the first London terminus for the GWR on a site next to the Grand Union Canal in Paddington.

The Eastern Counties Railway Company must have been keeping an eye on developments on the Euston Road, as in October 1835 the Board of Directors of the ECR resolved to build their terminus close to Bishopsgate, one of the main routes into the City of London from the north. The station would be ideally situated for bringing travellers and goods into

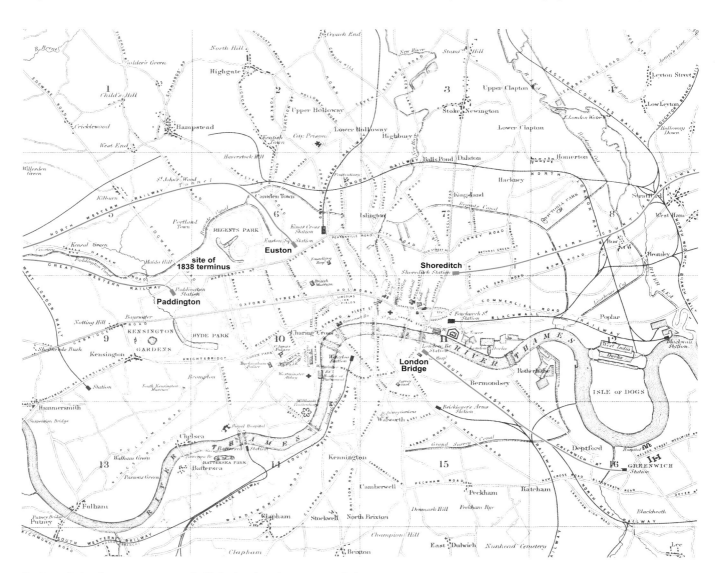

Fig 3 London's railway termini in 1840, highlighted on the index map to Stanford 1862

the commercial heart of London, but building a railway through the crowded streets of the East End would pose its own problems. The development of the railways took place in a haphazard way, as no local or national authorities sought to coordinate it.

Changing the landscape

The construction of the railways in the mid 19th century had a colossal impact on the fabric of towns and cities, far more so than the building of the canals less than a century earlier. In 1838 the impact of the construction of the London and Birmingham Railway on the urban and rural landscape was captured by the artist John Cooke Bourne (1814–96), and Charles Dickens was inspired by the gouging-out of the railway cuttings for the same railway through Camden to include this passage in *Dombey and Son*:

> The first shock of a great earthquake had, just at that period, rent the whole neighbourhood to its centre. Traces of its course were visible on every side. Houses were knocked down; streets broken through and stopped; deep pits and trenches dug in the ground; enormous heaps of earth and clay thrown up; buildings that were undermined and shaking, propped by great beams of wood. Here, a chaos of carts, overthrown and jumbled together, lay topsy-turvy at the bottom of a steep unnatural hill; there, confused treasures of iron soaked and rusted in something that had actually become a pond. Everywhere were bridges that led nowhere; thoroughfares that were wholly impassable … In short, the yet unfinished and unopened Railroad was in progress; and from the very core of all this dire disorder, trailed smoothly away, upon its mighty course of civilisation and improvement. (Dickens 1848, 78)

Before the arrival of the railways, travel was largely dependent on the natural contours and landscapes of spaces and places; the builders of railway lines were under no such restriction. Railway companies aspired to a perfect line, hard, smooth, straight and with a level gradient, which could only be achieved by changing the landscape with cuttings, embankments, tunnels and viaducts (Letherby and Reynolds 2005, 35).

Changing society

The railway was a key agent in altering perceptions of time and space, in that it made travel a less natural, human-scale phenomenon, speeding it up and changing perceptions of the landscape from the detailed to the panoramic. With the development of the railway, the act of travelling largely ceased to be an active part of the journey, with only departure and arrival as the real events (Letherby and Reynolds 2005, 7). In 1852, at a meeting of the Institution of Civil Engineers, Mr Braithwaite Poole marvelled at engines that were capable of drawing passenger trains at speeds of 60 miles an hour: 'In

course of time, passengers will probably be conveyed by the London and North Western Railway, from London to Liverpool, a distance of 200 miles, in four hours, or less' (Poole 1852, 459).

Fears were expressed not only about changes to the rural and urban landscape; politicians and social commentators were concerned about the impact that the railways, and the resulting mass mobilisation of the population, would have on the nation. The Duke of Wellington supposedly opposed the railways because they made the working class more mobile (Morriss 2003, 26), and it was a commonly held belief that the railways facilitated crime. The enclosed compartments of trains were convenient for murders and assaults, and trains could convey large groups of people to one place to commit mischief; in 1868 railway companies were banned from conveying rowdy crowds of boxing fans to prize-fights (Simmons 1995, 370–1).

The very presence of a railway in the locality was considered to be an agency for crime; at an inquest into the murders of two babies in Hammersmith in 1858, the coroner said: 'If there had been a railway in the parish, I should not have been so surprised' (Whitting 1965, 228). Dalston Junction station, on the NLR and one of the subjects of this monograph, was the location of a notorious, and desperately sad, railway crime. On 18 December 1899, Louisa Masset was found guilty at the Old Bailey of killing her 3-year-old son, Manfred, and hiding his body in the ladies' lavatories at Dalston Junction station (OB, t18991211-77). The court proceedings explain Masset's movements on the day of the murder, her journeys between the home of Manfred and his nurse in Tottenham, London Bridge station, Dalston Junction and Brighton, all facilitated by London's trams and railways. Masset was sentenced to death, and became the first person to be executed in Britain in the 20th century.

Building the railways

The construction of the railways brought large numbers of people, often unattached men, to parts of the country that were not necessarily equipped for their arrival. In rural areas, where there was no history of heavy industry, skilled workers and 'navvies' were brought in from elsewhere in the country. Without adequate housing and social facilities, it was thought, the itinerant workers would resort to alcohol and disorderly behaviour: 'The great amount of outlay already thus made, its suddenness, and its temporary concentration at particular localities, often spots before but thinly inhabited, have created or developed evils … touching both the welfare of the labourers employed, and the interests of society' (Select Committee of the House of Commons 1847, 4).

The fears of local communities regarding the influx of what were often presented as reckless, debauched drunks were expressed in contemporary accounts:

> The dread which such men as these spread throughout a rural community, was striking; nor was it without a cause. Depredations among the farms and fields of the vicinity were

frequent. They injured everything they approached. From their huts to that part of the railway at which they worked, over corn or grass, tearing down embankments, injuring young plantations, making gaps in hedges, on they went, in one direct line, without regard to damage done or property invaded … They often committed the most outrageous acts in their drunken madness. Like dogs released from a week's confinement, they ran about, and did not know what to do with themselves. (Francis 1851, 72–3)

A Parliamentary Select Committee was appointed to investigate the conditions under which labourers were employed in the construction of the railways and other public works, and in 1847 reported that 'the conditions under which their labour is carried on are too generally of a deteriorating kind … They are brought hastily together in large bodies; no time is given for that gradual growth of accommodation which would naturally accompany the gradual growth of numbers; they are therefore crowded into unwholesome dwellings, while scarcely any provision is made for their comfort or decency of living' (Select Committee of the House of Commons 1847, 6). The Select Committee drew attention to the inadequate housing provided for such workers, and the 'habits of indecency and discomfort' (ibid, 14) which remained in a community after the navvies had left. At the town of Lockerbie in Dumfriesshire (the population of which in 1847 was approximately 1400) over 600 railway labourers lodged in local houses, leading to severe overcrowding, which John Baird, the Clerk of the Peace for Dumfriesshire, believed was 'prejudicial to health and morals', as manifested in 'the drunkenness of the little boys, and the going together of men and women to live without marriage' (ibid, 16).

As a consequence, there came to be a market for the construction of temporary housing for railway workers, namely iron and timber dormitory buildings with communal dining facilities and separate kitchens, and the 'Labourers' Moral Cottage', which could be provided by Peter Thompson of Commercial Road, Limehouse, was designed with the nuclear family in mind, providing separate living and washing spaces, and bedrooms for parents and male and female children (Fig 4).

In the cramped East End, there was terrific pressure on undeveloped land, as there still is today, and there was insufficient open ground on which to build enough temporary housing for all the labourers engaged on the construction of the railways and other public works. The large numbers of workers who were drawn to London by the promise of work squeezed into tenements and lodging houses, causing the population of the city to explode. In 1851 the population of London was 2.3 million, but by 1911 it was home to 4.5 million people, or 7.3 million if the city's burgeoning suburbs are included (Morgan 2001, 529). In the late 19th century over 300,000 people lived in one-room tenements, and over 900,000 people were housed in illegal lodging houses or doss houses (Davies 2009, 15). The owners of lodging houses were required to register their names and addresses, and their

premises were regulated and inspected. They had to allow police inspections, keep their premises clean (giving immediate notice of the outbreak of infectious diseases), and limewash the walls and ceilings twice a year (ibid, 16).

The use of vacant plots of land for camping by itinerant labourers was not uncommon. Land in Flower and Dean Street, at the southern end of Brick Lane, had been cleared of its rookeries, or densely packed slum housing arranged around a maze of courts and alleys, following the Cross Act of 1875; the Home Secretary, Richard Cross, introduced the Act in order to challenge established slum districts by reforming housing provision. The land around Flower and Dean Street lay empty for two years while a dwellings company was found to develop the site, and the vacant plots were inhabited by itinerant tinkers and other travellers, to the annoyance of local businesses (White 2003, 21). Evidence from the excavations at the site of Bishopsgate goods station suggests that the vacant site may have been occupied prior to and during the construction of an extension to the station in the mid 1840s (Chapter 3.5).

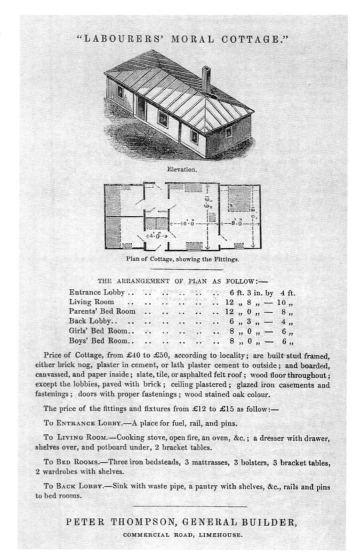

Fig 4 An advertisement for Peter Thompson's 'Labourers' Moral Cottage' (Select Committee of the House of Commons 1847, 45)

2.2 London's local railways

In 1853 the Metropolitan Railway and its competitor the Metropolitan District Railway (which later became the Metropolitan and District lines of the London Underground, respectively) were empowered to build an underground railway below the streets of the capital, connecting Paddington and King's Cross stations with the City. When the Metropolitan Railway opened in 1863, it was the first underground railway in the world. Further lines were built by competing companies, and by the end of the century much of central London's present-day Tube network had been constructed. The underground pioneered cheap trains for workers and in 1864 the Metropolitan Railway introduced early trains, for which return tickets cost only 3d, rather than the usual 9d. The introduction of special services and tickets for workers and commuters changed the shape of London; the construction of the railways had forced so many people from their homes, but the railways enabled a more scattered population to travel to work. The Great Eastern Railway was set up expressly to cater for those travelling to work; when in 1861 the GER was granted permission to construct Liverpool Street station, it was on condition that the company would run workers' trains from the north-eastern suburbs of Edmonton and Walthamstow into the City, with day return tickets costing 2d (Wolmar 2007, 134). Companies like the GER and the North London Railway were responsible for fingers of development springing up along the railway lines, focused around the locations of stations.

The construction of suburban railways brought the noise, pollution, shabbiness and squalor that had been feared by contemporary commentators even further into the towns and cities. In the 1870s, the NLR did not permit trains to run during Sunday church services, although cattle trains still ran, and engine drivers made 'such an infernal tumult with their shrieking whistles as to cause the service of the church to stop' (*The Builder* 29, 1871, 291, cited in Simmons 1995, 370). In 1903 residents living close to the NLR had 'been driven insane by that devilish screech and only wait an opportunity to shoot either the driver or the engine' (ibid, 370).

2.3 The railways in the 20th century

By the beginning of the 20th century, construction of a national network of railways, operated by different companies, was largely complete; the competition for business between lines which occupied a limited territorial space had almost reached saturation point, and smaller lines had not yet proved profitable (Letherby and Reynolds 2005, 24). Since the mid 19th century, railway companies had been merging with each other, or buying up smaller companies, in an attempt to maintain an advantage over their rivals; 1862 saw the amalgamation of the Eastern Counties Railway with several

other smaller companies to form the Great Eastern Railway, operating routes throughout East Anglia and even ferries to take goods and passengers from Harwich to the Continental ports of Antwerp, Rotterdam and the Hook of Holland.

The experience of greater cooperation between the train companies during the First World War, when the rail network was run by the Railway Executive Committee (comprising 11 managers of the biggest railway companies) led people to believe that there could be no return to the aggressive competition of the 19th century. The 1921 Railways Act sought to increase the national efficiency of the railway, especially as the motor car was becoming a serious competitor during the inter-war period. The 'Big Four' railway companies were created, each responsible for train services in a different part of the country: the Great Western Railway (GWR), the Southern Railway (SR), the London, Midland and Scottish Railway (LMS) and the London and North Eastern Railway (LNER), which absorbed the Great Eastern Railway along with several other companies. The years between the First and Second World Wars have been seen as the 'golden age' of the railways (Letherby and Reynolds 2005, 24), and the publicity departments of the 'Big Four' railway companies produced advertisements creating a 'romantic' image of train travel that persists today, if only in modern advertisements for train travel from London St Pancras to mainland Europe.

The Labour government elected in 1945, after the end of the Second World War, was committed to bringing the principal utilities, including the nation's railway network, into national ownership. At its formation in January 1948, British Railways was charged with providing an economical, integrated rail network that would break even, and a Modernisation Plan was published in 1955. The aim was to renew the infrastructure and equipment of the railways, including the eradication of steam locomotives, but the plans were never fully carried out. The former Technical Director of Imperial Chemical Industries (ICI), Dr Richard Beeching, was appointed as the first chairman of the British Railways Board in 1962, and at a time when road transport was becoming ever more popular and the car and road lobby was a growing force in the nation's economy, cuts were made in investment and unproductive lines were closed. Before Bishopsgate goods station was destroyed by fire in December 1964, its future was already the subject of some debate as the transport of goods by rail was in decline. Dalston Junction station closed in 1986, but had been in decline for some time before, with the bulk of the station building being demolished in the 1960s.

2.4 Railway infrastructure

The development of the railway network during the 19th century led to the construction of new kinds of buildings. The introduction of these new forms changed the shape of the rural and urban landscape, and introduced new opportunities.

The railway station was an entirely new kind of building within the urban landscape of the 19th century; long-distance travel for goods and people by road or canal predominated until the middle of the century, and passengers were collected from recognised stopping places such as coaching inns. There were no equivalent specialised buildings where one could buy a ticket, wait for a train in comfort, purchase refreshments and reading material, and dismount, possibly into a waiting horse-drawn vehicle, at the other end.

The proposed location of a railway station could be a matter of some contention; the City of London resisted the construction of railway termini, owing to the additional traffic that would impinge on the city's already overcrowded streets, and so London's earliest stations, at London Bridge, Euston, Paddington and King's Cross, were located on the periphery of the mid 19th-century city. This model was repeated elsewhere, and the terminus of the London and Birmingham Railway at Curzon Street in Birmingham, for example, was located on the edge of the city's core; but the construction of a railway station in the centre of a settlement could act as a catalyst for further development, as will be seen below in the context of Dalston (Chapter 6).

Many stations, from the mainline termini in London to provincial stations, were accompanied by hotels and refreshment rooms. The station at Swindon, on the Great Western Railway, opened in 1842 and was constructed by J D and C Rigby at their own expense. In return, the GWR agreed to stop all trains at the station for ten minutes so that passengers could take refreshments; Swindon was ideally situated at the mid-way point on the then four-hour journey between Bristol and Paddington, and was the only place where passengers could purchase food and drink, and avail themselves of other facilities, during their journey (Cattell and Falconer 2000, 36–7). The mad dash for the refreshments counter was depicted in Richard Doyle and Percival Leigh's *Manners and customs of ye Englyshe* of 1849 (Fig 5), and was the subject of at least one letter of complaint to the chairman of the GWR, Charles Russell:

We arrived at Swindon where we disbursed seven shillings and sixpence 'in no time' for pork pies and indifferent bottled malt liquor. One of my friends had an attack of indigestion on the road, and no wonder after such a meal … I may state that we all heartily deprecated the dictum that placed such beggarly fare before the public and said to them 'eat this or none, eat it up in less than ten minutes, and run to the train when the bell rings, as you will be left behind with nobody to sympathise with your inconveniences'… (TNA: PRO, RAIL 1008/34)

The railway infrastructure that might have had the greatest impact on the development of the urban landscape is the railway track, carried above the surrounding landscape on embankments and viaducts, or below the ground in cuttings and tunnels. Railway lines cut through existing geography and had a great impact on how the surrounding urban space functioned, as will be evident below from the examples of the viaducts of the Eastern Counties Railway and North London Railway (Chapters 4 and 6.2).

Fig 5 The dash for the refreshments counter during a break in a railway journey (Doyle and Leigh 1849, 40)

The railways had grown up primarily to transport goods, and even after railway companies developed their lines and stations mainly for passenger transport, the movement of goods continued to be an important source of income. Goods depots, yards and stations served to transfer goods between trains and road vehicles, and often incorporated warehouses for the temporary storage of goods; at Edinburgh Waverley, as at Bishopsgate goods station, the arches underneath the railway viaduct on the approach to the station were used for storage. Even small local stations would have a goods yard with a siding and goods shed where items could be removed from trains. Such separate facilities ensured that goods traffic did not interfere with that intended for the lucrative passengers, and separate goods yards were constructed for the shipment of coal, a heavy and dirty commodity which was required in immense quantity; the ECR and its successor companies maintained a separate coal depot to the east of Pedley Street.

The railway companies used large numbers of horses, as will be elaborated on later in this monograph, to shunt wagons and transport goods and luggage. Stabling was often constructed underneath railway arches or in purpose-built structures; for example, a multi-storey block of stables was constructed by the GER in 1881 in Hare Street, to the north of the Braithwaite viaduct on the eastern side of Brick Lane. A railway horse had a comparatively short life, of two years on average, and the railway companies sought to cater for the welfare of their horses by providing veterinary care at dedicated infirmaries, such as that at Pedley Street (Chapter 4.3).

The construction and operation of the railways created a great demand for housing; during the building of railway lines and stations workers were attracted towards the urban centres such as London, intensifying already crowded conditions. In rural areas temporary towns were constructed for the 'navvies', and at Swindon in Wiltshire the GWR built a new town to accommodate the skilled workers required by the company railway works. The new town included good-quality housing, schools, churches and social institutions; it was feared that without adequate housing, the good influence of families, and facilities for the improvement of minds, the workers would resort to drink and disorderly conduct, the kind of behaviour that was traditionally, and perhaps unfairly, associated with the less well-housed navvies. The ECR constructed a similar town to house those employed at its railway works in Stratford, to the east of London, and provided a hostel there for engine drivers and others who had to spend prolonged periods away from home. As the 19th century progressed, railway companies no longer took such a paternalistic attitude, and less accommodation was purpose-built for railway workers. The cottages of Roseberry Place in Dalston may not have been built to accommodate the railway workers of the NLR, but the census returns from the late 19th century indicate that many of the houses surrounding Dalston Junction station were lived in by those working on the railway, and their families.

The varying impacts that the coming of the railways to east London had on the urban environment and those who lived and worked in it, from the 19th century to the present day, will be explored in the following chapters.

3

Shoreditch below ground: archaeological evidence for clearance, and the construction of the Eastern Counties Railway

3.1 Weavers and tenements: Shoreditch before the railway

The area around Spitalfields, on the eastern side of the main route leading north from the City of London, has long been associated with the Georgian town houses of Huguenot silk merchants, but there existed another Georgian Spitalfields, further to the north; deliberately developed between the late 17th and early 19th centuries as an industrial suburb, it contained multiple occupation workshop tenements, predominantly for the weavers employed in London's silk industry.

The process of parcelling up and selling off the former estates of London's religious houses at the Reformation created several large freeholds on the northern side of the city, which were purchased by London merchants and lawyers including the Goddard, Wheler and Wilkes families; this created opportunities for speculative builders to develop the land for housing. Shoreditch and the northern side of Spitalfields never attracted the major freehold development that was seen elsewhere in London, such as the development of Mayfair and Belgravia in the West End. Instead, the landowners leased relatively small parcels of land on short leases to speculative builders who put up a few houses at a time. For example, by 1718 William Farmer, a local carpenter, had taken 61-year leases on plots of land on either side of Sclater Street, to the north of the future site of Bishopsgate goods station, and was building three-storey brick houses with cellars. Houses were often refaced, if not rebuilt, at the end of the lease (Guillery 2004, 89–90).

Silk working was one of London's largest industries during the 18th century, employing 10% of the city's working people, and the trade dominated Spitalfields, Bethnal Green and the eastern part of Shoreditch. Despite the silk trade being such a major industry, factory buildings were not constructed, in common with many other industries in London; building land was at a premium, and a purpose-built factory represented a substantial additional cost, especially when it would have stood empty during the night. Instead, dyed thread was 'put out' by masters to artisan weavers to weave in their own homes; these weavers were, officially at least, usually men, as only women who had been widowed were permitted to use looms under the ordinances of the Weavers' Company (Guillery 2004, 83). Masters collected the woven silk, often elaborate brocaded taffetas, satins and damasks, and sold it to mercers, the merchants who dealt in the trade in textiles. Weaving was carried out in houses that had been constructed in association with the growth of the silk industry in the 18th century, and were specially designed in order to accommodate the trade; the homes of weavers were not just domestic structures, but should also be understood as industrial buildings (ibid, 85).

Many different kinds of people were engaged in the weaving industry. These ranged from the poor journeymen who probably did not own their loom, and women and children, officially excluded from the act of weaving but who would engage in filling quills (the elongated unflanged bobbin that held the wound silk thread, and was inserted into a shuttle) or throwing a shuttle (passing the shuttle containing thread across the warp threads), to the highly skilled artisans. The common perception is that these artisans were more literate than others engaged in the weaving industry, and had a strong tradition of engaging in horticulture and keeping birds, 'to cheer their quiet hours when at the loom' (Edward Church, a Spitalfields solicitor, cited in Clapham 1916, 466). Such artisan weavers probably owned their own looms and earned enough to have stable households, attending the meetings of local historical, horticultural and musical societies, and forming 'an intensely orthodox community, intelligent, skilled and enlightened within limits but, on the whole, generally anxious to be accepted as "gentlemen"' (Rothstein 1987, 136).

In any case, there was a great contrast between silk producers, who eked out a subsistence living, their lives and living conditions dominated by work, and the consumers of the fruits of their labours. The materials for a silk dress might cost about £50, more than two years' wages for an artisan weaver (Guillery 2004, 86).

Much of the housing stock in the north of Spitalfields, eastern Shoreditch and Bethnal Green was purpose-built for multiple occupancy, with each floor of a building consisting of a single tenement. The earlier silk merchants' houses of Spitalfields were later divided up into single-room tenements, and it was within such rooms, both adapted from older properties and purpose-built, that 'a man has his loom in his room and sleeps in it with all his family' (the Society for Preventing Contagious Fever, 1817, cited in George 1925, 192). Taking a train from the newly opened Shoreditch station in 1841, Charles Knight described how the train cut through a 'densely populated mass of buildings', where

> house after house presents, at the upper stories, ranges of windows totally unlike those of common dwelling-houses, and more nearly resembling those of a factory or a range of workshops … in which every house without exception possesses these wide, lattice-like windows, more frequently at the upper than the lower part of the house … it is not difficult to detect here and there indications of the frame-work of a loom, and of woven substances of different colours. The windows tell their own tale; they throw light upon the labours of the Spitalfields weavers, who, almost without exception, inhabit the houses here spoken of. (Knight 1841, 385–6)

The Spitalfields Act of 1773 introduced regulation of weavers' wages and provided an element of protection for the trade; further Acts of Parliament prevented the import of foreign silk, and silk masters resident in London were not permitted to employ weavers living outside the city – though with the high concentration of skilled workers in the area and Spitalfields' proximity to the docks, silk masters may not have wished to relocate anyway (Guillery 2004, 88). Regulated wages did, however, lead purchasers of woven silk to procure it from communities of weavers residing outside London; Spitalfields witnessed its last boom in the early years of the 19th century, as silk-weaving centres in Essex, Macclesfield, Coventry and Paisley prospered. The Spitalfields Acts were repealed in 1824, allowing foreign imports of silk into London; the resulting

poverty and 'distress' of Spitalfields' weavers caught the attention of the nation, and directed the zeal of reformers who published descriptions of the area's unending misery (ibid, 88).

Religious dissent has long been a characteristic of Shoreditch and Spitalfields; first by the Huguenots against the established Catholic (in France) and Anglican (in England) Churches (Guillery 2004, 87), setting the pattern of a local acceptance that extended to eastern European Jews in the 19th century, and Bangladeshi and Bengali Muslims in the 20th century. The long history of dissenting against the establishment manifested itself in the Calico Riots of the early 18th century and continued acts of defiance during the economic fluctuations in the silk industry, and has perhaps also been at the root of social unrest in the 20th century, in the form of Jewish anarchism and socialism, and ongoing battles against the British Union of Fascists and the National Front.

3.2 Demolition of tenements prior to the construction of the Shoreditch railway terminus

There were three main phases of demolition associated with the construction and expansion of the Shoreditch railway terminus and the Eastern Counties Railway (Fig 6). The land on which the Eastern Counties Railway Company built their railway line and terminus (B:B51; below, 3.3) in Shoreditch at the end of the 1830s lay within the parishes of St Leonard Shoreditch at the western end, St Matthew Bethnal Green on the northern side, and Christchurch Spitalfields on the southern side. The land was bought from the post-Dissolution landed estates of the Goddard, Wheler and Wilkes families, who began to develop the land by parcelling it up and leasing it to speculative builders on short leases, as described above (3.1). The Goddard family estate included the Stone House, which was leased to William Goddard by the prior of St Mary Spital in 1534, and stood to the east of Shoreditch High Street; the house and surrounding land was developed for housing as Webb's Square and Goddard's Rents from the 17th century onwards. The estates of the Wheler and Wilkes families comprised the south end of Cock Hill, the north end of Wheler Street, Farthing Street, the north side of Phoenix Street, Bell Court, Elizabeth Court, Vine Street, King Square and part of the western frontage of Brick Lane, much of which was either bought by the ECR in the late 1830s or was later swallowed up by the construction of Bishopsgate goods station (below, 3.8).

The buildings on the eastern side of Shoreditch High Street, from No. 40 to No. 53, were also purchased by the ECR, together with the Badger's Court warehouse and Bryant Street (Sheppard 1957, 27, 100, 112, 252; ERO, D/P 134/28/1; HAD, M7612). The buildings were then demolished by early 1841 (HAD, M698, p 78; TNA: PRO, HO 107/694/7, fos 26–38). This row of buildings is shown in Tallis's street view (Fig 7), drawn between 1838 and 1840, at the very moment when the

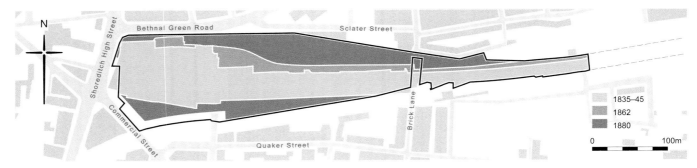

Fig 6   Schematic plan showing the three main phases of demolition in Shoreditch in advance of the railway (scale 1:5000)

Fig 7   The buildings that were originally located in front of Shoreditch station, shown in Tallis's street view of 1838–40 (Jackson 1969, 155 part 59)

buildings on the eastern side of Shoreditch High Street were being purchased and demolished.

The inhabitants of the houses had to be moved, further increasing the population density of the area (Mander 1996, 61); and while landowners were compensated for the loss of their land, tenants were not.

The laying out of the railway line was held up by the crowded and insanitary nature of the area through which it was required to pass, the foundations of the viaduct piers having to be dug through basements, cesspits, sewers and ditches (Bird 1922, 252). In Bethnal Green, Braithwaite's viaduct of 1840 cut across Lamb's Fields, an area of boggy ground 700ft (214m) long, into which the privies of surrounding houses drained; according to a Dr Southwood Smith, 'there is always a quantity of putrefying animal and vegetable matter, the odour of which, at the present moment, is most offensive' (cited in Gavin 1847, 22). The construction of the ECR reduced the size of this area of ground, but no attempt was made to clean it up, and the pollution was instead confined and concentrated within a smaller area; adjacent to the viaduct, for 'a distance of about 230 or 250 feet, and from forty to sixty feet in width, was one enormous ditch or stagnant lake of thickened putrefying matter; in this Pandora's box dead cats and dogs were profusely scattered, exhibiting every stage of disgusting decomposition' (ibid, 23).

At the western end of the site, adjacent to Shoreditch High Street, evidence of activity dating back to the 11th and 12th centuries was found during the recent excavations, including a shallow ditch and a group of brickearth quarries. During the 13th century, occupation was focused along Shoreditch High Street, and remains associated with the late medieval property Stratton House, dating to the 15th century, were found. Evidence was also found of demolition, robbing of stone and building materials, and rebuilding throughout the 17th and 18th

centuries, a time when plots of land to the east of the High Street were being parcelled up and leased out to local builders for the small-scale development of workers' housing.

Nos 49–51 Shoreditch High Street

John Tallis's street view (Fig 7) suggests that at the time of its demolition, 50 Shoreditch High Street (B:B41, Fig 8) was a three-storey building, three bays in width, with a garret and a double bow-fronted shop on the ground floor; on a stone set into the brickwork was inscribed 'Three Wheatsheafs TGA 69' (HAD, M698, p 78), perhaps referring to a period of refurbishment or rebuilding when 50 Shoreditch High Street was owned by the Timmings family, during the mid to late 18th century (LMA, MR/PLT 5717–30). A side entrance door was situated on the southern side of the shop (Jackson 1969, 158–9 part 59), and 49 Shoreditch High Street (B:B44) was located to the south (Fig 8). Archaeological evidence suggests that, prior to the demolition of buildings and structures on the eastern side of Shoreditch High Street, the area had gone into decline. The surveyors of the ECR had condemned the quality of buildings in the area, and their conclusions were reflected in the archaeological evidence. The neat 18th-century brick floors, thought to have been internal to 49 and 50 Shoreditch High Street (B:B44 and B:B41 respectively, Fig 8), were overlain with a series of external make-up deposits and rough surfacing layers (B:OA66, Fig 8). These rudimentary surfaces were constructed in an ad hoc fashion, using brick, cobbles and numerous other types of reused building material. The tenement buildings were systematically demolished in direct response to the construction of the railway, and the land these buildings occupied reverted to open area, external yard space. Cesspits occurred within these later external yard surfaces, suggesting the continued use of nearby surviving dwellings. One such pit was cut into the former brick floor surface associated with 50 Shoreditch High Street (B:B41) (not illustrated). The recently demolished buildings were also truncated by later robbing trenches and one of these episodes (B[2057], Fig 8) can be dated to *c* 1820–60 by a small quantity of mostly factory-made crockery, which includes a complete pot lid from a small pot of cold cream (<P1>, Fig 9). The lid has transfer-printed decoration in black, depicting a basket of flowers together with the name and address of the perfumer:

HENRY BURTON / OTTO OF ROSE COLD CREAM / 18 GREEK ST SOHO / LONDON (Pearce 2009). The overall process of the demolition and extraction of building materials was likely to be taking place for a while after the opening of the ECR's Shoreditch terminus and also with the construction of Bishopsgate goods station (B:B39; Fig 8 and Chapter 4.6).

To the north of 50 Shoreditch High Street (B:OA63, Fig 8), a brick-lined box drain was recorded which produced pottery suggesting that it went out of use between 1845 and 1895. The

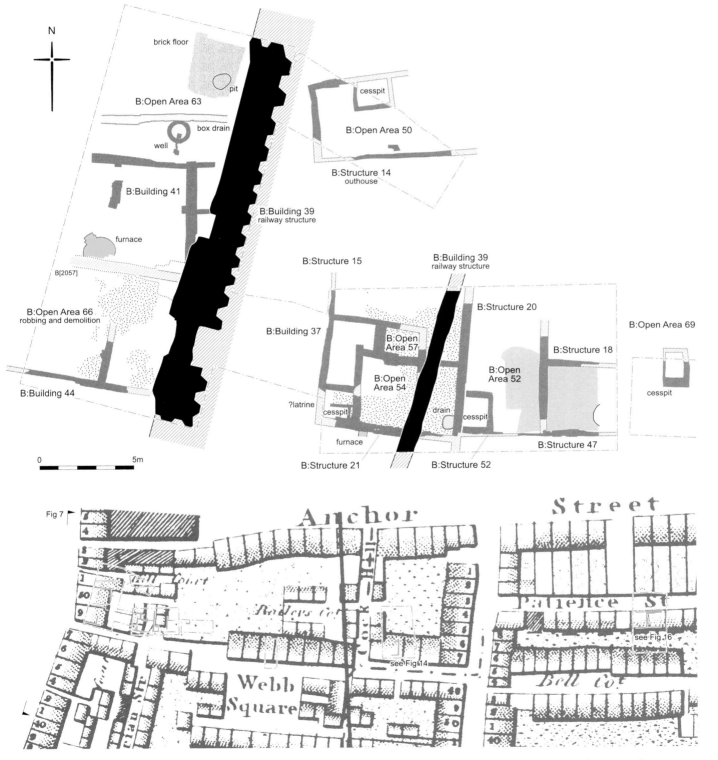

Fig 8 Demolished buildings, structures and open areas at the western end of site B, Bishopsgate goods station (scale 1:200); lower – projected on Horwood's 1799 map

<P1>

<P2>

Fig 9 Refined whiteware (TPW3) pot lid <P1> from demolition spread B[2057], with black transfer-printed decoration and the name and address of the perfumer Henry Burton (scale 1:1)

Fig 10 English stoneware (ENGS) blacking paste pot <P2> from demolition spread B[738] (scale 1:1)

slightly later dating for the disuse of this feature could be attributed to the fact that well-constructed drainage features such as this can often be retained by later landowners. A single-storey row of shops was constructed on the eastern side of Shoreditch High Street to screen the entrance forecourt of the railway terminus, and the drainage features may be associated with this land use. These shops were demolished in the late 1870s when Bishopsgate goods station was constructed.

No. 51 Shoreditch High Street is also depicted in Tallis's street view of 1838–40 (Fig 7) as a three-storey building with a garret and a double bow-fronted shop on the ground floor. A low entrance on the northern side of the shop led to seven cottages arranged around Hill Court to the east (Jackson 1969, 158–9 part 59). In the period prior to ECR demolition, in 1818 and 1820, Samuel Forsaith insured a school room and seven houses in Hill Court, all of which were constructed of brick and timber. In 1834 the occupiers of No. 51 were Charles Pitt, a staymaker, and a pastry cook (GL, MS 11936/541, no. 1184866).

Plots to the rear of 49–51 Shoreditch High Street

To the east of these properties, a number of foundation walls belonging to different phases of building (B:S20, B:S21, B:S15, B:S47, B:S52 and B:S18) bounded a group of enclosed yards (B:OA54 and B:OA57 (west) and B:OA51 and B:OA52 (east)) (Fig 8). A brick-built soakaway and two cesspits were found here; Horwood's map of 1799 (Horwood 1813; Fig 8) suggests that the cesspits would have been used by the occupants of the tenements that had been constructed in this area by the end of the 18th century. The foundations, or semi-basement, of a small L-shaped building, possibly a latrine (B:B37, Fig 8), were excavated, and pottery from the infill (B[738]) of the building dates its demolition to between 1807 and 1830. Among the utilitarian wares found within the rubble was a complete English stoneware (ENGS) blacking paste pot (<P2>, Fig 10; cf Green 1999, type 427, 171). The blacking of the fire grate was an important task in the Victorian household, and these sturdy

pots are relatively common finds on sites in London.

The abandonment fills, B[723], of a cesspit in Open Area 54 (B:OA54, Fig 8) contained a large quantity of clay pipes, pottery and other household objects which combine to indicate that infilling took place in the 1840s, an event therefore linked to ECR demolition. Discarded in varying condition, the 148 pottery vessels (reconstructed from 348 sherds and weighing 13,344g) are mostly mismatched blue transfer-printed pearlware (PEAR TR) teacups dating to the period 1810–30, with well-known and popular designs such as 'Dresden flowers', and various other floral and landscape patterns. After the printed wares, a significant proportion of the food preparation and serving vessels discarded in this pit is yellow ware (YELL), a durable, heavy-duty, mass-produced fabric made in the north of England from the 1820s, which becomes increasingly common in London a decade or so later. Evidence of dining crockery is slight, restricted to a few plain creamware (CREA) plates and pearlware (PEAR) plates with either rococo or evenly scalloped blue shell-edged rims (cf Miller et al 2000). Instead, YELL and CREA rounded bowls with mocha or banded industrial slip decoration (cf Sussman 1997 for description) are more common, suggesting that the consumption of quick semi-solid meals was important. Filling out the picture of everyday family life, among the more intimate objects is a nursery mug with a printed moralising motto, now incomplete, reading 'LOVE YOUR CHILD … GOD … BOOK … SCHOOL' (Pearce 2009). Completing the group are a number of well-preserved chamber pots in plain CREA and YELL with mocha or banded industrial slip decoration.

Among the other rubbish discarded here was a large group of 42 clay tobacco pipes dating to 1840–80 and notable for their well-smoked and burnt character. Among the few identifiable pipe makers are Thomas Balme of Mile End (operating 1805–45: Oswald 1975, 132) and the Leach family of Whitechapel (1844–69: ibid, 140–1), with pipes decorated with symbols related to a public house, such as the Fox and Grapes, Spread Eagle, the Turk's Head and the Horse and Hounds, also being represented. In addition, there are a number of worked animal bone finds, namely an openwork bone fan rib <S1>, of high-quality workmanship, a spoon <S2>, a whistle <S3>, presumably intended for a child, and a conical tapering tube <S4>. The latter, possibly for attaching hosing, may have had a medicinal purpose (Egan 2009).

Historic maps, such as Horwood (1813), depict the spread of domestic activity eastwards from Shoreditch High Street. Further evidence for tenement plots, most likely situated within Hill Court according to the map data, was identified during the excavations (Fig 8). A series of brick wall foundations delineated a rectangular structure (B:S14) that may represent the remains of an outbuilding or store. A rectangular cesspit (B:OA50) was recorded adjacent to the north wall of the structure, supporting its interpretation as an outhouse.

Slightly further south-east within Open Area 69 (B:OA69, Fig 8), 46 pottery vessels (reconstructed from 131 sherds and weighing 3188g) were retrieved from the disuse deposit of a cesspit (B[171]). The material appears to represent the everyday crockery owned by a single household during the second quarter of the 19th century (Fig 11). It is notable that only pottery was discarded here, with the other rubbish commonly found in similar features of this period, especially tobacco pipes and glassware, being absent. Representing a better-preserved and more coherent pottery assemblage than that found in cesspit B[723] (in B:OA54, above), blue transfer-printed pearlware (PEAR TR2) teacups, saucers and slop bowls (eg <P7> and <P8>, Fig 11) dating to the period 1810–30 dominate, decorated with a variety of idyllic views of the British countryside, with a few refined whiteware plates and a tureen decorated with the ubiquitous willow pattern print providing tableware crockery. Pearlware with industrial slip decoration (PEAR SLIP) also features, with a further slop bowl and barrel-shaped jug (<P9> and <P10>, Fig 11) representing the better-preserved elements of this group. Completing this discrete crockery assemblage are a number of well-preserved refined white earthenware (REFW) chamber pots, including a complete example (<P11>, Fig 11).

The archaeological sequence to the east of Shoreditch High Street becomes increasingly complex from the 17th century onwards. Numerous phases of construction, often directly overlying each other, have been identified and reflect increased competition for space in a rapidly expanding suburban part of London. In some instances, pre-existing wall lines had been rebuilt, added to, and incorporated into later structures and buildings. Differential survival, owing to truncation by the construction of Shoreditch station in the 1830s and 1840s, and later of Bishopsgate goods station, has somewhat hampered interpretation of the site.

Nos 52 and 53 Shoreditch High Street

Nos 52 and 53 Shoreditch High Street were both three-storey two-bay buildings with a garret and a shop at the time of their demolition in c 1840 (Fig 7). In 1828–30, John Spiller had a bakery at No. 52, and in 1835 C Voaz had a china and glass warehouse (Robson 1830; 1835). The entrance to Swan Yard lay under No. 54, to the north (Jackson 1969, 158–9 part 59). In addition to insuring the brick and timber school room and

houses in Hill Court (above), in 1818 and 1820 Samuel Forsaith also insured 52 and 53 Shoreditch High Street and their contents.

The use of the western end of site B during the 13th century was focused along the frontage of Shoreditch High Street, and was attested by occupation-related features, although the earliest structural evidence dated to the latter part of the 15th century. These remains are likely to be associated with the late medieval property, Stratton House. Demolition, robbing and rebuilding were witnessed throughout the 17th and 18th centuries.

Cock Hill

In the 16th century, Cock Hill, or Cock Lane, had been bordered to the west by Swan Orchard and to the east by Lompitts, an area of land $1^{1}/_{2}$ acres (0.6ha) in size and used as a tenter ground, where newly manufactured cloth would be stretched taught on frames to dry after fulling. In the 1670s, John Nichol purchased the freehold on $4^{1}/_{2}$ acres (1.8ha) of land, including ground to the north of Cock Hill, and subsequently leased this to Jon Richardson, a mason, with a permit to dig the ground to make bricks (Wise 2008, 14). Brick making was usually a local affair, as the significant cost of transporting bricks made manufacture close to the city a necessity, and Richardson's brickfields were ideally placed for the expansion of Spitalfields during the late 17th and 18th centuries.

The southern end of Cock Hill was purchased by the Eastern Counties Railway in 1839 for redevelopment as the Shoreditch railway terminus. By 1841 there were four houses on the eastern side of Cock Hill, in close proximity to the recently completed station, and these were occupied by six families whose heads worked as weavers, a dealer, a shoemaker and a dyer (TNA: PRO, HO 107/694/7, fo 38). Two of the houses (including a shop) on the eastern side of Cock Hill were in the ownership of Hannah Edwards in 1846 (PA, HL/PO/PB/3/plan 1846/E41).

3.3   The Shoreditch railway terminus

The next chapter will summarise the results of standing building recording undertaken on the site of Bishopsgate goods station and the Braithwaite viaduct in Pedley Street, to the east of Brick Lane. This section will deal with the below-ground archaeological evidence for the construction and development of the building which pre-dated Bishopsgate goods station, and was one of the earliest train stations in the capital, the Shoreditch railway terminus.

The construction of the Eastern Counties Railway

The Eastern Counties Railway was intended to link the capital with Norwich, and was initially promoted as the Grand Eastern Counties Railway; a prospectus with a map of the projected course of the railway was published in August 1834, and included estimates of construction costs by the company

Fig 11 Ceramic finds from cesspit fill B[171]: plain yellow ware (YELL) deep-flared bowl <P3> and yellow ware pitcher with industrial slip decoration (YELL SLIP) <P4>; Nottingham stoneware (NOTS) cup <P5>; pearlware saucer with underglaze blue-painted decoration (PEAR BW) <P6>; pearlware saucer and slop bowl with type 2 blue transfer-printed decoration (PEAR TR2) <P7> and <P8>; pearlware rounded or slop bowl with industrial slip decoration (PEAR SLIP) <P9>; PEAR SLIP barrel-shaped jug <P10>; plain refined white earthenware (REFW) chamber pot <P11> (scale line 1:4, photographs 1:2)

engineer John Braithwaite and of projected revenue by Mr I C Robertson, who later became the company secretary (Goslin 2002, 5). The 'Grand' part of the title was dropped before the Bill for its construction was introduced in the House of Commons on 19 February 1836. The Bill received stiff opposition from landowners and the promoters of two rival groups who wanted to build railways in the area, but this was overcome and on 4 July 1836 the ECR received the Royal Assent (Allen 1975, 1–2).

The directors of the ECR were initially keen that their line be constructed in a similar manner to Isambard Kingdom Brunel's Great Western Railway, on a broad track gauge of 7ft 1/4in, rather than the standard gauge of 4ft 8in; this would give passengers a smoother ride and allow trains to run faster. The company engineer, John Braithwaite, felt that this would prove too costly, and the idea was dropped. As there was initially no intention of making any physical connections with other railway lines, Braithwaite instead suggested that the tracks could be laid with a non-standard gauge of 5ft, and this was duly accepted.

The ECR was beset by financial problems. The line was planned to run from London to Norwich, but the project ran over budget, and all the money that should have been used to construct the full length of the line was instead spent on the stretch between London and Colchester. More money had to be spent on the purchase of land than had been anticipated, and as the line passed through a largely agricultural district, relatively little revenue was generated by carrying goods into the city; a railway connecting industrial areas might have paid larger dividends (Knight 1851, 848).

A second company received the Royal Assent to construct a railway on the same day as the ECR; the Northern and Eastern Railway aimed to connect London with the towns of Bishops Stortford and Hertford to the north, and the promoters originally envisaged that they would have their own City terminus. Lack of funds ruled this out, so before construction the ECR and N&ER reached an agreement; the two railway lines would join at Stratford, and share the line and the terminus at Shoreditch. As a result, the N&ER had to conform to the 5ft gauge (Allen 1975, 1–2), but by 1844 it became clear that a non-standard gauge would impede future development of the companies, so both railway companies converted all tracks, trains and rolling stock to standard gauge.

Plans of the proposed route of the railway were drawn up in 1835 to accompany the Bill (Fig 12). These show that the site of the railway terminus in Shoreditch High Street was to cover an area that encompassed Briant Court, Briant Street, Sheerings Alley and Webb Square, and that the viaduct which carried the railway line into the station would be built on land which at that time was occupied by buildings on the northern side of Phoenix Street. A survey of the area of Shoreditch through which the railway would be built was undertaken late in 1835:

... from a point adjacent to Brick Lane, where it was originally proposed that the Eastern Counties Railway should terminate, as far forward as High Street, Shoreditch, for a breadth of two hundred feet, that this space included not more than 373 houses of which 140 were very old and consisted of two rooms and let to weekly tenants at sums varying from 2/6d to 3/6d each. 130 are four and five roomed houses in a most ruinous state. 50 are larger but equally ruinous and not more than 30 are in a good state of repair or of much value. (Minutes of the Provisional Committee of the Eastern Counties Railway, 22 October 1835)

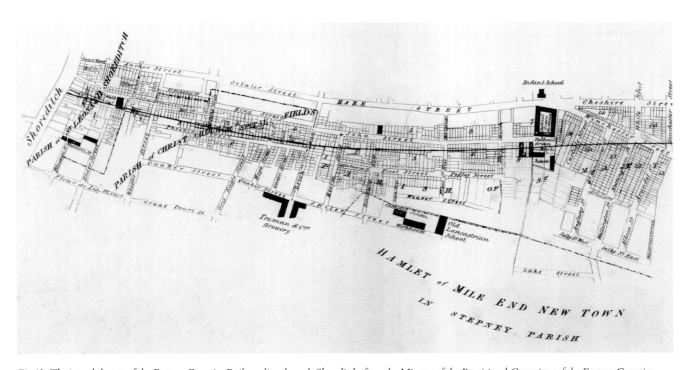

Fig 12 The intended route of the Eastern Counties Railway line through Shoreditch, from the Minutes of the Provisional Committee of the Eastern Counties Railway, 22 October 1835 (TNA: PRO, RAIL 186/2)

The construction of the line began in March 1837 (*GER Magazine* 3, 1913, 115). Most of the land and property purchases for the terminus and final stretch of line through Shoreditch were made in 1839 and 1840 (BR (Eastern Region) Great Eastern deeds S/2, cited in Sheppard 1957, 252).

The owners of properties demolished for the construction of the ECR were compensated for their loss, but tenants were not. More than 50 years later, the authorising Act of 1887 for the extension of Liverpool Street station insisted that those displaced by the demolition and construction works had to be rehoused at the expense of the railway company. Ten purpose-built blocks of model dwellings were erected to accommodate 600 of the 737 people displaced by the extended railway station (Connor 2000, 34).

The ECR began operating on 18 June 1839; the line ran from Romford in Essex (now part of Greater London) to a temporary terminus at Devonshire Street, Mile End, with intermediate stations at Ilford and Stratford (*VCH* 1966, 22). Construction of the western end of the viaduct and the terminus at Shoreditch continued, and the station opened at the western end of the present site on 1 July 1840; the Devonshire Street station was subsequently closed and later demolished. The N&ER began their services in September 1840, and work on the station continued until at least the autumn of 1842. At first the railway companies only carried passenger traffic, as there were no freight facilities at Shoreditch, but in 1840 and 1841 two small goods stations were opened by the ECR and the N&ER, to either side of the mainline into the Shoreditch terminus at the eastern end of St John Street (later renamed Grimsby Street), and to the east of Fleet Street Hill. The depots (both known as Brick Lane goods depot) expanded quickly during the early years of the railways, and by the 1850s there was a large general goods depot on the northern side of the railway line, fronting on to Hare Street (later renamed Cheshire Street). The goods depot on the eastern side of Fleet Street Hill was later renamed Spitalfields goods station.

Building Shoreditch station

The design, construction and development of Shoreditch station will be discussed further in Chapter 4.2, but the passenger terminus was an Italianate Classical stone building designed by the company engineer, John Braithwaite. It contained five sidings, between platforms 250ft (76.2m) long, and also incorporated separate facilities for the Northern and Eastern Railway Company. The station was raised on a series of brick arches, with a semicircular court at the west end flanked by ramped approach roads for carriages on the north and south sides, and staircases for foot-passengers. The railway line entered from the east on a viaduct 1¼ miles (2.01 km) long from Mile End, consisting of 160 arches varying in span from 36ft to 62ft (10.97–18.89m) between massive brick piers. From 1846 the terminus was called Bishopsgate station. Some of the arches between Wheler Street and Brick Lane were leased out to greengrocers (Sheppard 1957, 252–4; Anon 1847, 4, 7; *The Builder*, 28 December 1844, 638–9).

Despite its large size, owing to the truncation caused by the massive foundations required by Bishopsgate goods station the archaeological evidence for the construction of the Shoreditch railway terminus (B:B51) was slight. Structural evidence for the Shoreditch terminus was limited to a fragment of its northern external wall, aligned east–west. To the east of this structure, a large foundation aligned north–south represented a foundation beam for a ramped road which was located on the northern side of the station building (Fig 13; Fig 14). This ramp allowed horse-drawn carriages (and as shown in Fig 15, a bicycle whizzing down the ramp) to access the ticket office, waiting rooms and departure platform. The ground level of these buildings was truncated by the construction of Bishopsgate goods station (B:B39), which opened in 1882.

Although the railway development did not directly impact the tenement buildings on the northern side of King Street until the demolitions associated with the construction of Bishopsgate goods station, there is evidence to suggest that there was not a static occupation. During the early 19th century Building 18 was demolished, and by the time of the construction of the Open Area 79 goods yard the rears of the tenements had reverted to an open yard containing two circular brick-built cesspits. By the latter half of the 19th century the cesspits within this open area had fallen into disuse and were truncated by the construction of the latest building, not related to railway activity, constructed on the site (B:B28).

While the arrival of the ECR had a significant impact on the buildings, and people, standing in its path, the tenements on Patience Street and King Street to the east could be considered to have been largely unaffected, structurally at least, by this initial phase of railway development.

Fig 13 The foundation of Shoreditch railway terminus (B:B51) truncating the cellar of a tenement building (B:B5), looking north (0.5m scale)

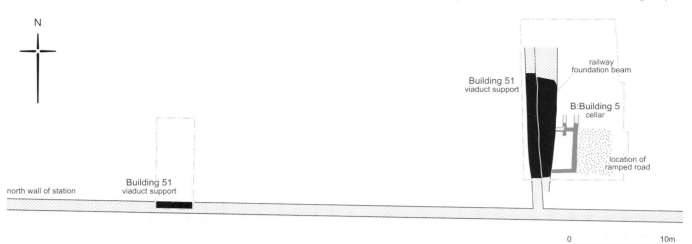

N

0   10m

Building 51
viaduct support

railway
foundation beam

B:Building 5
cellar

location of
ramped road

north wall of station

Building 51
viaduct support

Fig 14 Plan showing the northern wall of Shoreditch railway terminus (B:B51) and the foundation of the carriage ramp (scale 1:750)

Fig 15 Bishopsgate (formerly Shoreditch) railway terminus in 1862, with the carriage ramp on its northern side (City of London, London Metropolitan Archives, SC/PHL/02/627 74/13851)

3.4 Railway expansion: tenement demolition and the first goods yard

In 1846 an extension to the station was planned to provide more facilities for passenger traffic and a small goods yard, necessitating the purchase of more land in 1848 (Sheppard 1957, 253; Anon 1847, 6). It was proposed to widen Braithwaite's viaduct on its southern side, crossing over Phoenix Street, Quaker Street, Wheler Street, Farthing Street, Grey Eagle Street, Hope Street, Queen Street, Brick Lane and George Street. Parts of these streets were acquired, along with a further section of the frontage of Shoreditch High Street, part of the southern side of Anchor Street, the remainder of Cock Hill, Patience Street, Pullen's Court, Little Patience Street and much of King Street

(ERO, Q/RUm 2/46; PA, HL/PO/PB/3/plan 1846/E41). In November 1847 a contract was awarded to T and W Pipes, builders, for work to be undertaken at what had by then been renamed Bishopsgate station, including the construction of new waiting rooms and platforms, the coke platform, turntables and travellers, and the engine drivers' house. The contract included excavating and filling, and digging and ramming postholes, while vaults 44 and 45 underneath Braithwaite's viaduct of 1840 were to be fitted up as stables and paved (TNA: PRO, RAIL 186/92).

The demolition of Patience Street

In the 1840s, prior to its demolition, weavers still predominated among the working families who lived in Patience Street (Fig 8, lower; TNA: PRO, HO 107/694/7, fos 25v–27v), which had been in existence since the 1680s and formed part of the estate of the Byde family. Archaeological evidence for occupation in the street dated to the late 17th century, with the further construction of tenements in the 18th and early 19th centuries.

Pullen's Court, also known as Pullman's Court or Pullen's Buildings, was entered from an opening between 5 and 6 Patience Street and contained six small houses, extending into the parish of Christchurch Spitalfields to the south. Pullen's Court was built by Joseph Pullen, the leaseholder of the small plot of land on which it stood, during the early 19th century (PA, HL/PO/PB/3/plan 1846/E41). Pullen was a builder who lived at 40 Old Castle Street in Bethnal Green (LMA, MJ/SP/1834/07), and with his wife Martha kept a lodging house at 10 Collingwood Street, also in Bethnal Green (OB, t18340515-81). A chandler's shop in Old Castle Street was kept by someone of the same name, either Pullen himself or a relative (LMA, MJ/SP/1834/03). Pullen was representative of many small-scale speculative builders in east London, often bricklayers, carpenters and other tradesmen, who leased small parcels of land from remote landowners in order to construct a few houses at a time. The rapid population growth that London witnessed in the decades after 1800, when the number of Londoners grew by 100,000 or more each decade, created a huge pressure on housing in the city; sites were developed more intensively than they had been in the past, some by 'speculative builders of the most scampy class' (*VCH* 1998, 124) who constructed dwellings with no foundations, poor timber and half-burnt bricks on the former rear yards and gardens of existing houses. The construction of the extension to the passenger terminus, and of the later Bishopsgate goods station, truncated much of the remains of Pullen's Court and of buildings on the southern side of Patience Street. In 1836, following Joseph Pullen's death, his executors insured the houses in Pullen's Court and the 18th-century tenement buildings at 5 and 6 Patience Street (GL, MS 11936/552, no. 1236023). In 1841

No. 6 was occupied by the sawyer Edmund Page and his family (TNA: PRO, HO 107/694/7, fo 26). The 1841 census return for the neighbouring Little Patience Street is incomplete; three houses are listed but the only occupation noted among the residents is that of a wood turner (TNA: PRO, HO 107/694/7, fo 28).

The cellars of 6 and 7 Patience Street (B:B8 and B:B7 respectively; Fig 16; Fig 17) were excavated, and the finds recovered from the basement of 7 Patience Street are considered below.

No. 7 Patience Street

In 1841, 7 Patience Street (B:B7) was occupied by the carver George Knight and his 15-year-old son, who was a cabinet apprentice (TNA: PRO, HO 107/694/7, fo 26v). The backfill of the cellar (B[1266]) of this property contained a large quantity of objects, in particular ceramics and clay tobacco pipes mostly dating to the first quarter of the 19th century. With No. 7 known to have been demolished much later, it is likely that this material was imported from a nearby source and cannot therefore be considered as solely representative of the material culture used by the final occupants of this property. Nevertheless, a flavour of the materials discarded here and description of any unusual items retrieved is given below.

The pottery includes part of a bedpan with a well-formed, non-spill, inturned rim (<P12>, Fig 18). The vessel would have had a long tubular handle opening into the interior, allowing the contents to be emptied with the minimum of unpleasantness. Bedpans, stool pans and chamber pots formed an important part of the potter's repertoire in the 18th and 19th centuries, and potters from the Surrey-Hampshire borders are known to have maintained contracts to supply hospitals and other institutions in London with such necessary wares into Victorian times (Bourne 1920). The use of bedpans is associated with invalids and the bed-ridden, while chamber pots were in everyday use in an age before household sanitation needs were met by the widespread use of water closets.

A range of utilitarian bowls and dishes were found in the demolition rubble of 7 Patience Street, among them various serving and condiment vessels. These include half of a brown-glazed Surrey-Hampshire border redware (RBORB) double condiment dish (<P13>, Fig 18). The small carinated bowl, glazed inside, was one of a pair originally luted together but now separated, and was probably made in the late 18th century. The remains of at least ten creamware (CREA) dinner plates were found, as were various teawares, mugs, dishes and an eggcup. A creamware (CREA PNTD) cream or milk jug is decorated with Chinese-style figures, one holding a parasol, among trees, painted in low-temperature colours over the glaze (<P14>, Fig 18), and a near-complete pearlware (PEAR SLIP) table salt cellar was also found (<P15>, Fig 18).

Part of a rounded English porcelain bowl (<P16>, Fig 18), produced at Worcester (ENPO WORC) and decorated with the popular 'bat' print, was also found in the demolition layers of 7 Patience Street. The slightly violet-tinted blue and washed-in effects painted by hand are associated with production at

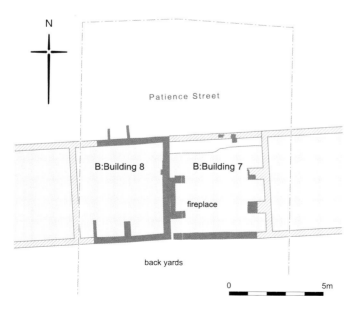

N

Patience Street

B:Building 8   B:Building 7

fireplace

back yards

0   5m

Fig 16 Plan showing demolished tenements on Patience Street (Nos 6–7) (scale 1:200)

Fig 17 Excavation of 6 and 7 Patience Street, showing the floor surface, fireplace and later cesspit at No. 7, looking south-west

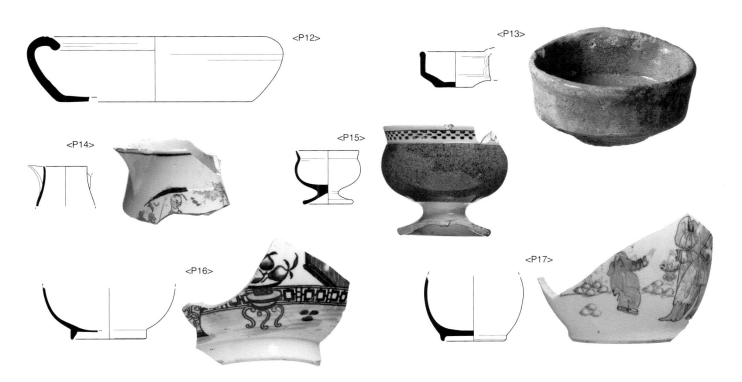

Fig 18 Ceramic finds from B[1266], demolition infill of 7 Patience Street: Surrey-Hampshire border redware with brown glaze (RBORB) bedpan <P12> and condiment dish <P13>; creamware with polychrome painted decoration (CREA PNTD) milk or cream jug <P14>; pearlware salt cellar with industrial slip decoration (PEAR SLIP) <P15>; Worcester porcelain bowl with blue transfer-printed decoration (ENPO WORC TR) <P16>; Chinese porcelain vase with famille rose decoration (CHPO ROSE) <P17> (scale line 1:4, photographs c 1:2)

Worcester in the last quarter of the 18th century, and the bowl is best classed as a 'bason', a waste or slop bowl, intended as part of a tea service, the smaller examples of such vessels holding a quarter of a pint (Godden 1969, 29). A Chinese-style disguised numeral is printed underneath the base; comparable marks were found on sherds excavated from the Warmstry House site, where Worcester's first porcelain factory was situated. English porcelain is far less common on the Patience Street site than Chinese wares, a pattern repeated across London in the 18th century. Most of the Chinese porcelain (CHPO) from the demolition rubble of 7 Patience Street is decorated in blue and white, but there is also the lower part of a jar decorated in *famille rose* palette (<P17>, Fig 18). The painting is of fine quality, and the surviving portion depicts a man and a woman, one of whom offers a basket to a child who is reaching out for its contents.

Also found within the demolition rubble B[1266] was a bone shuttle <S5> for tatting, a technique used for the manufacture of durable lace; thread would be wound on to the shuttle, which facilitated the making of lace by hand (Beeton 1870). Lace was traditionally a luxury item, but had become a more widely available material as its manufacture by machine became common during the early 19th century. The counties of the south Midlands, namely Oxfordshire, Buckinghamshire, Bedfordshire and Northamptonshire, were centres of mechanised lace-making, and 'most lace was produced under circumstances far different from the image most people hold in mind: that of well-dressed, genteel ladies exhibiting their femininity through their prowess at the delicate art of lace-making' (Beaudry 2006, 151). Across the country, lace making by hand employed large numbers of women, children and some men for long hours, and was an important cottage industry, especially given that – under the protections offered by Weavers' Company ordinances – the women of Spitalfields and Shoreditch (with the exception of widows) were not permitted to use looms (Guillery 2004, 83). Informal engagement in allied trades such as lace making, suited to the well-illuminated weavers' tenements of the area, may have been common, but would not necessarily be visible in the census records of the 19th century.

No. 24 Patience Street

To the east of 6 and 7 Patience Street (B:B8 and B:B7), the demolished remains of a further tenement at 24 Patience Street (B:B46) were excavated. The structural remains of the building were very fragmentary. Only an east–west aligned external load-bearing wall and an internal partition wall aligned north–south remained, and this latter wall was partially robbed following demolition. Pottery recovered from the demolition backfill (B[262]) is dated to *c* 1840–1900, although it also contained a high proportion of 17th-century pottery.

Building 15 to the east of 24 Patience Street was also demolished to make way for the extension to Bishopsgate passenger station. Structurally all that remained was an east–west aligned section of its northern external wall and a fragment of its internal area to the south. As with the buildings to the west, enough survived to suggest that the latest brick floor was

partially dismantled or robbed prior to its backfilling. The demolition backfill (B[1831]) is dated to *c* 1820–50 (Pearce 2009). A white tin-glazed wall tile <T1> was also recovered (Betts 2009), as well as a fragment of ivory waste <S6>, possibly for a button (Egan 2009). Further evidence of tenement buildings (B:B17), albeit heavily truncated, was located to the east.

Buildings 9 and 14 were the remains of tenements which stood on the northern side of Patience Street, the latter adjacent to the junction with Little Patience Street. Building 9 was constructed during the population explosion of the early 19th century; at the time of Horwood's survey of the area in 1799 (Horwood 1813), the northern side of Patience Street was occupied by the rear yards and gardens of the buildings in the street immediately to the north, Anchor Street (later Sclater Street).

At the intersection of Patience Street and Little Patience Street stood the surviving remains of Building 14, comprising a fragment of its east–west aligned southern external wall and the remnants of a robbed brick floor. The demolition dumps (B[1812] [1813]) are dated after 1844 by the presence of the clay tobacco pipe <CP1> made by Bernard Leach (Grey 2009a). Among the remaining 44 pipes discarded in this deposit (some of which had been well used and are heavily scorched) are ones by local pipe makers, including <CP2> made by Robert Osborne of Shoreditch in 1836–45 (Oswald 1975, 142).

The pottery from B[1813] is dated earlier by a decade or so and is characteristic of vessels used in the late Regency to early Victorian household. These include two stoneware ginger beer bottles and a small conical pot for blacking paste, used to clean the cast iron fire grate or cooking range. The assemblage also features sherds with transfer-printing, with plates with the 'wild rose' blue-printed pattern being most common. It also contains two imported vessels, one of them undoubtedly residual but included here on account of its considerable rarity on excavated sites in England. This is part of a small Dutch red earthenware (DUTR) brazier (<P18>, Fig 19), of the kind frequently depicted in 17th-century genre paintings from the Netherlands. It has a carinated profile and convex tripod base, but the rim has been formed into a square in plan. Glazed inside and out, the vessel would originally have been handled and was used to hold burning coals or charcoal as a form of portable heating that was frequently employed by smokers. Examples are extremely rare in London excavations, and it appears that the form was not generally used in the capital.

Fig 19 Dutch red earthenware (DUTR) brazier <P18> from demolition infill B[1813] of Building 14 (scale 1:2)

3.5 Expanding the railways: the goods yard of the 1840s

The burgeoning popularity of the railways in the mid 19th century was manifested in the need for the Eastern Counties Railway to construct a dedicated goods yard on the northern side of the Shoreditch terminus, only a few years after the railway first opened in 1840. Evidence for this mid 19th-century expansion was present in the form of three brick-built structures. The most substantial of these was Structure 32 (Fig 20), thought to represent a pier base or the foundations for one of the subsidiary rail tracks which diverged from the mainline into the goods yard. It comprised seven equally spaced (north-east to south-west aligned) brick-built foundations. It was constructed from a mixture of dark red brick, probably from local brickfields in London, and yellow London stock bricks which were brought in from north Kent and south Essex. Pottery associated with its construction is dated at the latest to c 1820–50.

Further related structures were situated to the east. An east–west aligned wall (B:S34) is thought to have formed the northern boundary wall of the goods yard, along what was the southern frontage of King Street. A partially exposed 0.8m deep triangular brick structure (B:S33) was located to the south, but its function is not clear. It is not visible on the 1st edition Ordnance Survey map of the area of 1872, where this particular area is crossed by the additional rail lines (Fig 21).

One of the largest features excavated on the site was a

Fig 20 Foundation beams from Structure 32, looking east (1.0m scale)

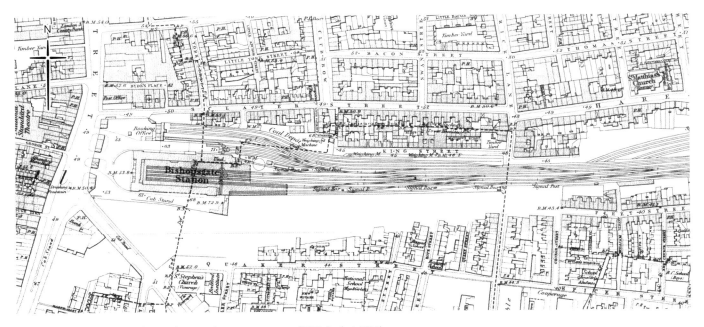

Fig 21 Bishopsgate station on the 1st edition Ordnance Survey map of 1872 (scale 1:2500)

possible sand quarry (B:OA79) which, owing to its considerable depth, could only be partially excavated; it had a timber structure surviving on its southern side (Fig 22). The pottery recovered from the infill of the quarry dates to between 1830 and 1846, and it may be inferred from the dating evidence that the quarry was opened immediately before the construction of the goods yard to the north of Bishopsgate passenger terminus, and perhaps served the construction process.

Not all of the evidence found within Open Area 79 was industrial in nature, and a number of post-demolition cesspits were identified within the area of the demolished tenements. One unlined example was cut through the demolished remains of Building 7; while the feature was stratigraphically later than the demolition of the building, the pottery assemblage contained within its backfill (B[1310]) is dated to 1807–30. This feature yielded an eclectic range of materials such as cloth offcuts <S7>, but included a lot of iron ranging from a quantity of wire <S8>, structural fittings in the form of a bolt <S9> and door handle <S10>, to a ring <S11> for lining barrels and fragments of lining from wooden boxes <S12>, as well as a composite wooden handle <S13> and a gun flint <S14> (Egan 2009). In addition to the typical everyday kitchen and household crockery of the period, a near-complete dish in oriental porcelain, probably from Korea, was also found (<P19>, Fig 23). It has blue-painted decoration and an unglazed ring inside the base, and represents an extremely unusual find in London.

Fig 22 The southern edge of the possible sand quarry (B:OA79), showing the timber bracing, looking south (1.0m scale)

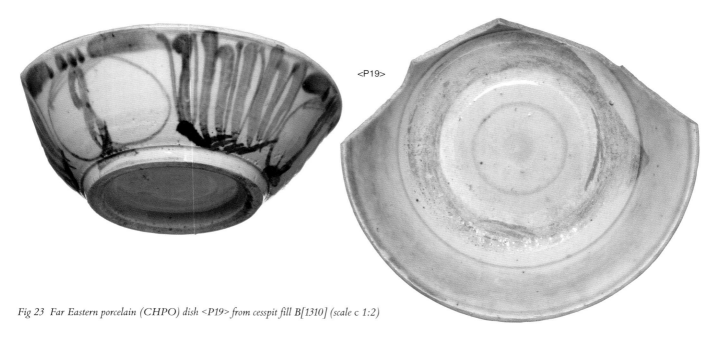

<P19>

Fig 23 Far Eastern porcelain (CHPO) dish <P19> from cesspit fill B[1310] (scale c 1:2)

Fig 24 *An unlined cesspit between the foundations of Structure 32, looking north–west (1.0m scale)*

The disuse (B[1312]) of a second unlined cesspit to the south located between two of the foundations or footings of Structure 32 (Fig 24) in Open Area 79 is dated by fragmented pottery to *c* 1825–50. The adoption of the north-east to south-west alignment suggests that the cesspit post-dated the construction of Structure 32, although its disuse, as suggested by the dating evidence, would have occurred relatively shortly afterwards. Another unusual object came from the cesspit fill, part of a small pipeclay figure (<P20>, Fig 25) in the form of a male figure dressed in costume typical of the 1680s holding a tipstaff, and bearing a close similarity to part of a pipeclay figure found on a site to the south of Aldgate High Street in

1974 (site code AL74: Weinstein 1984, fig 60). This example is clearly residual or was carefully curated for many decades before it was discarded, probably when broken (Pearce 2009). Other finds included a bone spoon <S15>, presumably belonging to a child. A small assemblage of food waste consisting entirely of chicken bone was also found.

The Ordnance Survey map of 1872 (Fig 21) shows that this activity occurred within an area marked as a coal depot, which contained a weighing machine. The construction and use of cesspits after the demolition of tenements and other buildings suggests that the site may have had a more unofficial use immediately before and during the construction of Shoreditch station's goods yard, as an example of a cleared area being used by vagrants or navvies.

<P20>

Fig 25 *Continental pipeclay figure <P20> from cesspit fill B[1312] (scale 1:1)*

3.6 Redevelopment on King Street

During the 19th century, King Street was home to a constantly shifting population of poor working families who lived in overcrowded conditions. In 1841 No. 3 was in multiple occupancy by four families whose members were working as a labourer, silk weavers and winders, chair makers and a harness maker (TNA: PRO, HO 107/710/1, fo 5v). The property is not listed in later census returns, and in 1847 it was noted as having been pulled down (GL, MS 6008A/7). Also in 1841, No. 9 was in multiple occupancy by four families, members of which were working as a general dealer and silk weavers (TNA: PRO, HO 107/710/1, fo 7v). No. 10 in 1841 was likewise in multiple occupancy by three families working as cabinet makers and weavers, and with one of the sons being an apprentice maker of looking-glass frames (TNA: PRO, HO 107/710/1, fo 8).

Not all the buildings were in multiple occupancy in 1841, and 8 King Street was occupied by Henry Elliston, a cabinet maker, and his family (TNA: PRO, HO 107/710/1, fo 7). A decade later, in 1851, the same building was, however, in multiple occupancy by four families of a brush maker and silk weavers. One visitor was a maker of artificial eyes (TNA: PRO, HO 107/1543, fos 228v–229).

An equally diverse range of professions is represented in the census records of 1851 for 9 and 10 King Street. Four families were living in No. 9 in that year, working as a hairdresser, a laundress, a slop worker, a labourer, a tailoress and a silk weaver (TNA: PRO, HO 107/1543, fo 229). The silk weavers, who had appeared in the area with the arrival of Huguenots in 1685, following the promulgation of the Edict of Fontainebleau which banned Protestant worship in France (Scouloudi 1987), were finally disappearing in the 1860s. The census of 1871, the final one before the demolition of the northern side of King Street, shows that there were three families with members working as a horse keeper, laundresses, a labourer and a carman residing in No. 8 (TNA: PRO, RG 10/505, fo 5), while in No. 9 there lived a boot maker, a chair carver and a paper colourer (TNA: PRO, RG 10/505, fo 5v). A wood cutter, a wood turner, a trimming weaver and a charwoman were professions recorded in the census records for 10 King Street (TNA: PRO, RG 10/505, fo 5v).

To the west Building 47, situated along with its rear yard on the northern side of King Street, and Building 48, constructed in the 18th century, were maintained without any structural alteration, as was Building 35, a tenement also on the northern side of King Street, the frontage of which was truncated by the retaining wall for Bishopsgate goods station. Open Area 68, located on the northern side of the intersection of King Street and Brick Lane, defined to the south by Structure 38, was still in existence. On the Ordnance Survey map of 1872 (Fig 21) Open Area 68 is recorded as a timber yard.

An exception to the archaeologically apparent status quo was represented by the creation of Open Area 61, its subsequent disuse and the construction of Building 28, an ancillary railway structure. The yard (B:OA61) was located over the demolished and robbed remnants of Building 18, a tenement building constructed in the latter part of the 17th century (Pearce et al in prep); a bone fan <S16> and evidence of bone working <S17>–<S20> (Egan 2009) were found scattered within the yard. Two intercutting brick-lined cesspits were cut into this surface along with a number of associated slot features relating to the wooden privy shed that once covered them. The disuse infilling B[527] of one of these cesspits is dated to c 1845–65 by the particularly rich group of ceramics discarded. This discrete group totalling 87 vessels (reconstructed from 309 sherds and weighing 8057g) comprises the usual range of kitchen (red

earthenware bowls) and household coarsewares (a stoneware ginger beer bottle, and plain whiteware stool pan and serving dish), as well as a large quantity of transfer-printed pottery in blue and other colours. Blue-printed wares include a few heavier-bodied gothic panelled or facetted cups decorated with the 'Rhine' print. Matching crockery was also available to set the table for meals. The occupants used a number of plates decorated with the 'Hyson' print in blue and which also bear the printed mark of Joseph Clementson (Godden 2003, cat no. 910a, 150) who operated from Shelton, Hanley in Stoke-on-Trent (Staffordshire) in 1839–64. The presence of pottery by the same maker and with the same print suggests that these items were brought together with aesthetic considerations in mind. In addition, the few matching decorated teacups and saucers of bone china painted in the Chinoiserie style (Davis 1991) would have been marketed as the higher end of household china. Two figures would have been displayed as ornaments. Both are in polychrome painted pearlware (PEAR PNTD); one consists of the head and feet only (<P21>), but the other is the figure of a woman wearing a poke bonnet and a bright, royal blue surcoat (<P22>, Fig 26). Her face is delicately painted in flesh colour with pink cheeks and framed by black hair, and details of her clothing are picked out in gold (Pearce 2009). Little in the way of other rubbish was discarded here, with just a few clay tobacco pipes of the same date as the crockery recovered.

The final evidence of development on site B prior to the final demolition episode associated with the construction of Bishopsgate goods station during the late 1870s was represented by Building 28 (Fig 27). This building represents construction during an intense period of 19th-century activity in this part of King Street. It was built of brick on a cemented foundation. Pottery associated with its construction is dated at the latest to c 1850–1900. A possible entrance to the building was located to the north-east. While the function of the building is unclear, we can say that it was a relatively short-lived structure, being demolished, robbed and truncated with the construction of the Bishopsgate goods station some 25–35 years later.

<P22>

Fig 26 Polychrome painted pearlware (PEAR PNTD) female figure <P22> from cesspit fill B[527] (scale 1:2)

Fig 27 View of Building 28 under excavation, looking north-east (0.5m scale)

3.7 Nos 2–3 St John Street and 105 Brick Lane

To the east of Brick Lane, the site of the Pedley Street viaduct lay within a largely rural landscape (known as Great and Little Hare Marsh) until the 18th century. The natural springs in the immediate area of the site are documented as having supplied water via conduits to the medieval hospital of St Mary Spital to the south. The vicinity was also used from the Tudor period for activities such as brick making, giving its name to Brick Lane, and in the 17th century the Civil War defences of London extended into the area. Urbanisation spread east of Brick Lane from *c* 1700; Rocque's map of London of 1746 (Fig 28) indicates that at that time the site was situated on the edge of London, with dense settlement to the west, towards the main arteries of Bishopsgate and Shoreditch High Street, whereas to the east of Brick Lane were areas of open ground and market gardens; the Greenwoods' map of London of 1827 (not illustrated; Greenwood and Greenwood 1827) shows that the site was gradually infilled with buildings, and it had become largely built up by the mid 19th century (Fig 29).

The 1841 census suggests that 2 and 3 St John Street were inhabited by tradesmen employed elsewhere. These included John George, a 55-year-old labourer who was residing at 3 St John Street. John had five children, ranging in age from his daughter Ann, a weaver, and the eldest at 30, to another Ann aged 3 – quite possibly the eldest daughter was gravely ill at the time of the younger Ann's birth, prompting the family to give the newest member the same name. His son William, a weaver aged 28, lived at No. 2, which was shared with the Brown family. By the time of the 1851 census John, now aged 65, had turned No. 3 into an 'eating house' and his son, still residing at No. 2, had ceased to be a weaver and become a fishmonger instead. A third family, the Waits, were also living at No. 2 in 1851.

In the 1861 census John, aged 74, is recorded as an 'eating house keeper' and his son William as a now 46-year-old 'retired fishmonger' residing with him at No. 3. William was married but had no children, and his wife, appearing in the 1851 census, is not recorded in that of 1861. The 1871 census return records that 3 St John Street stood empty, although No. 2 was still an eating house – at that time, however, being run by the Padley family, comprising William, his wife Mahala, and their 2-month-old son Henry. The house was also home to five other residents, namely one servant and with the Padleys supplementing their income by renting rooms to four boarders. Interestingly, by 1881 No. 2 is empty and No. 3 has become the eating house, still run by William Padley. The buildings were demolished soon after in order to construct the short stretch of railway viaduct in St John Street, which was renamed Grimsby Street in 1909.

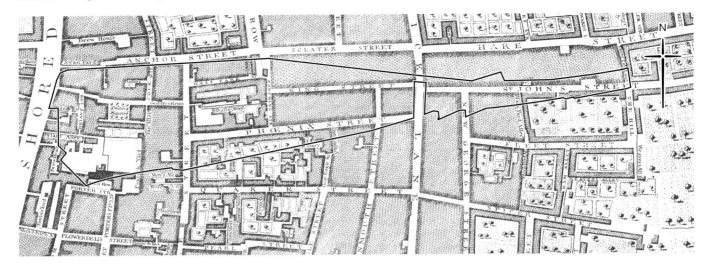

Fig 28 John Rocque's map of London of 1746, showing the area later occupied by the Eastern Counties Railway and Shoreditch station

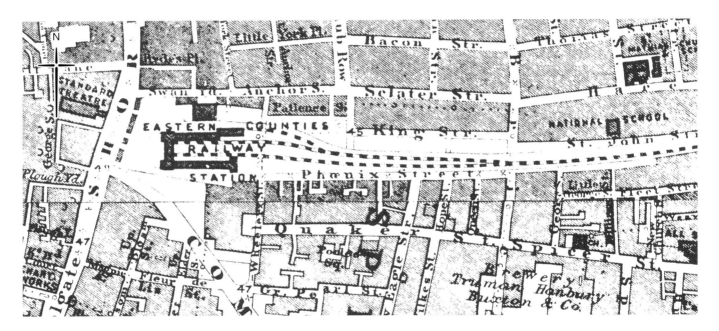

Fig 29 The Eastern Counties Railway and its terminus in Shoreditch High Street on Stanford's map of London of 1862

To the west of 2 and 3 St John Street, 105 Brick Lane appears to have been a beer shop during the middle of the 19th century. In the 1841 and 1851 censuses beer retailers are recorded within the premises, and although it is possible that these people did not sell from the building, its subsequent uses would suggest that it was already a shop. In the censuses of 1861 and 1871 it is clear that the building was in use as a coffee house, by 1881 it (like 2 St John Street) stood empty, and by 1891 it was no longer recorded. The relationship between the coffee house at 105 Brick Lane and the eating houses to the east in St John Street is uncertain. Although the two properties are not directly linked by person, it is intriguing that a coffee house and eating house operated side by side for almost the same period of time in the mid to late 19th century.

Archaeological remains represented the foundations of 2 and 3 St John Street (C:B1) which were constructed in *c* 1680

(Birchenough et al 2009) in the open ground known as Hare Marsh. Activity preceding the suburban development in the area investigated was represented by pitting, a curvilinear ditch and east–west aligned cart-ruts. The archaeological evidence, married with the environmental evidence, suggests increasingly boggy conditions in that area which necessitated the deposition of a rubble raft prior to the construction of the buildings (C:B1). The buildings were constructed free-standing, with dump levelling deposits raising the ground to form St John Street immediately to the south. A cellar was located to the west, while to the east deposits again raised the ground level.

Building 1 underwent two further building phases after its initial construction. The first included the replacement of the internal cellar wall with a new slightly off-centre retaining wall; an aperture in the new wall may represent an entrance to the cellar. A similarly aligned wall to the east was constructed at the same time. These building alterations are thought to have occurred towards the latter part of the 18th century, although their exact dating could not be ascertained. The second building alteration programme is thought to have taken place during the early 19th century, and comprised a partial deepening of the existing cellar floor level to the south. This was facilitated by the construction of a single-skinned wall underpinning the previously noted internal retaining wall.

All of the finds associated with disuse of the building were recovered from the demolition infill C[1] and internal deposit C[2] located in the cellar compartment (2 St John Street). The disuse and demolition of the building can be dated to the period after 1863 by a Victorian halfpenny (<S21>) found in the cellar infill. This links the assemblage from site C back to the Padley family and their eating house, with the material culture found in the cellar supplying a range of objects one associates with such premises. Clay pipes smoked by the customers of the eating house were common finds within the cellar infill (Grey 2009b), and include examples marked with the initials of local makers such as Thomas Leach, who was active in 1858–67 in Whitechapel Road (<CP3>), and William Walker, who operated in 1834–60 from Wheler Street, Spitalfields (<CP4>). Though some pipes pre-date the eating house, all had been smoked before being discarded, with some showing heavy use with smoke staining, but none are burnished and none are of the highest quality, suggesting that they were not smoked by people of a high socio-economic status. Only one pipe is a 'fancy' decorated example, bearing the feathers of the Prince of Wales (<CP5>); the remainder are more simply decorated with leaves or ears of wheat running down the seam of the bowl. Also found were a glass condiment lid (<G1> and <G2>), possibly from a mustard pot, and part of a press-moulded glass salt cellar (<G3>) used for food seasoning.

Objects relating to the consumption of soft drinks at the eating house include a complete green glass bottle, probably for mineral water, and two complete stoneware ginger beer bottles, in addition to the sherds from two others. Heavier-bodied blue transfer-printed refined whitewares include three well-preserved saucers all decorated with the 'Rhine' print, in addition to a few transfer-printed refined whiteware saucers with 'flow blue' decoration. The main feature of the pottery (Blackmore 2009) is the concentration of 22 sherds from eight custard cups mostly decorated with the same print. Until the early 19th century, custard was often served in its own right as a part of a sweet course (Coysh and Henrywood 1984, 100), but it was also considered a suitable food for invalids, and was made according to a range of recipes which at their richest might include 12 egg yolks to each pint of cream (Whiter 1978, 121). A range of forms was made for storing and serving custard, the latter including handled glasses and ceramic cups, some lidded. They also included large lidded pails for storage, small straight-sided jars (butter tubs) and a variety of cups, all lidded and several with stands, in some cases fixed, or as an integral part of the cup; some were made as sets with a ceramic tray (Savage and Newman 2000, 91). The number of 19th-century custard cups

here is of interest as they are rarely found on excavations in London; other examples are from Upper Thames Street in the City of London (site code UTA87), Goswell Road in Islington (GSW90) and Lot's Road School in Chelsea (CAU08). The custard cups from GSW90 were linked to the Victoria Coffee Rooms at 169 Goswell Road and its proprietor Samuel Martin in the 1840s and 1850s, with the range of other pottery (including yellow ware pitchers and whiteware willow-pattern printed cake plates) and glass used there supplying an insight into how this coffee house was furnished. To date the eating house assemblage recovered from site C represents only the second group found in London. The first, excavated from Borough High Street, Southwark (218BHS83, context [11]), is related to John Hinton's tenure, who furnished his premises with matching green transfer-printed plates and bowls bearing his name and address (96 Blackman Road, later Borough High Street) in print in panels on the rim; the crockery is otherwise decorated with the 'Sicilian' print.

The only other objects discarded in the former St John Street cellar at site C are of a more personal nature and were presumably owned by a member of the Padley family or their servant and boarders. They comprise a bone toothbrush <S22> and a copper-alloy comb fragment <S23> (Richardson 2009).

3.8 The Bishopsgate goods station

The construction of Bishopsgate goods station (B:B39), which opened in 1882, marked the culmination of 19th-century railway development on the site, and was the latest in a sequence of almost 900 years of human activity in Shoreditch and Spitalfields. The construction of the goods station's substantial foundations had truncated many of the earlier structures and deposits on the site, and a brief summary of the internal features related to its construction and usage is provided below. The remains are referred to in relation to their designated vault number.

The majority of the archaeological investigations on the site were located within the individual vaults of the lower level of Bishopsgate goods station. The only exception to this was the westernmost trench which was located on the western frontage of the goods station (Fig 30). Each vault, with the exception of vault 51, was bounded by substantial north–south aligned viaduct pier bases built in brick. These were constructed on substantial foundations which extended up to a metre either side of the stepped brick footings.

A narrowing of the basement in the eastern end of Building 39 was represented by an alignment of retaining walls which formed the internal northern limit of the basements in this part of the building. These were identified in vaults 22 and 24. The floor surfaces or roads observed beyond the extent of the vaults were constructed from large granite cobbles.

Subsurface remains relating to the goods station consisted of ceramic pipedrain runs found in vaults 29, 36 and 38. In vaults

Fig 30 The retaining wall in trench 10 (B:B39), looking east

36 and 38 soakaways and downpipes in the centre of the floor slabs channelled water to ceramic drains located on the eastern side of the vaults. A brick-lined sewer or conduit was identified in vaults 22 and 24.

<S24>

Fig 31 Incomplete bone pin or needle <S24> from deposits associated with the construction of Bishopsgate goods station (B:OA83) (scale 1:1)

A large quantity of material was recovered from the construction deposits associated with the goods station, with much of this material derived from truncation and disturbance of earlier truncated remains. This artefactual evidence was, perhaps as would be expected, diverse and contained much residual material, including personal items such as a bone pin or needle (<S24>, Fig 31). Large quantities of clay pipes (eg <CP6>, Fig 32), pottery (eg <P23>–<P25>, Fig 32; Fig 33) and building material were also found associated with the construction of the goods station. There was evidence for children's toys in the form of a very small, complete bone china teapot (<P26>, Fig 34) which was probably part of a doll's set (Pearce 2009). A somewhat less innocent artefact is represented by an iron bayonet <S25> (Egan 2009).

Structural materials found in the construction deposits associated with the goods station included bricks, peg- and pantile roofing tiles and a number of tin-glazed wall tiles. Four decorative tiles with different designs were found within the construction deposits; these depict a mounted soldier (<T2>, Fig 35), two landscape designs and a biblical scene. A decorated mid 16th-century tin-glazed floor tile from Antwerp was also present (<T3>, Fig 35), along with a later London or Dutch medallion floor tile showing the hindquarters of a dog (<T4>, Fig 35).

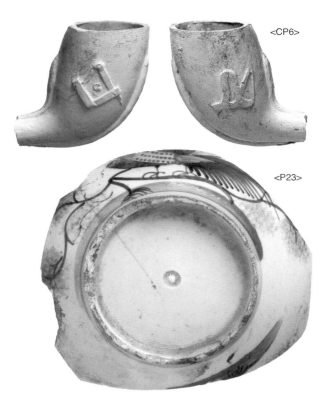

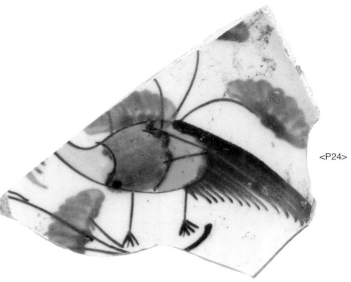

Fig 32 Ceramic finds from deposits B[682] associated with the construction of Bishopsgate goods station (B:B39): masonic clay pipe <CP6> dated 1850–1910, with bowl clasped by claw (scale 1:1); pearlware with underglaze polychrome painted decoration (PEAR PNTD) teacup <P23> and saucer <P24> (scale 1:1)

Fig 33 English stoneware miniature mug with Bristol glaze (ENGS BRST) <P25>, from deposits B[2117] associated with the construction of Bishopsgate goods station (B:B39) (scale 1:1)

Fig 34 Bone china toy teapot <P26>, from deposits B[523] associated with the construction of Bishopsgate goods station (B:B39) (scale 1:1)

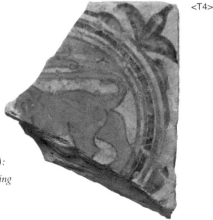

Fig 35 Tin-glazed tiles from deposits B[523] associated with the construction of Bishopsgate goods station (B:B39): tile depicting a mounted soldier <T2>; mid 16th-century floor tile from Antwerp <T3>; medallion floor tile showing the hindquarters of a dog <T4> (scale 1:2)

3.9 Conclusion

Within 50 years, the suburban landscape of this part of Spitalfields and Shoreditch had contracted, to be replaced by the expansion of the railways and associated industrial activity; entire streets, yards and courts were demolished, and communities removed, in advance of the construction of Bishopsgate goods station.

At the eastern end of the site, adjacent to Shoreditch High Street, there is evidence to suggest a decline in occupation at the time of the construction of the adjacent railway terminus, as the buildings which had been constructed on former rear yards went out of use and were demolished.

4

The development of the Great Eastern Railway and its associated structures

4.1 Before the railway

The previous chapter summarised the results of archaeological excavations which took place on the site of the former Bishopsgate goods station (site B), and which revealed evidence for the buildings which stood in the area between Shoreditch High Street and Brick Lane, and the lives and occupations of those who lived in them. These buildings were demolished in order to build the Eastern Counties Railway's Shoreditch terminus, and during the later construction of Bishopsgate goods station. This chapter will examine the above-ground archaeology associated with the site, the standing structures built by the railway companies, and the impact they had on the development of Shoreditch and the lives of the people living there.

4.2 Shoreditch station: the Eastern Counties Railway terminus

Railway station design was a subject of some debate, as companies tried to accommodate the conflicting needs of passengers and goods. In the 1830s and 1840s, the railway station was a new kind of building, where new kinds of activities took place: 'buying books, newspapers, socks and greetings cards, and any type of food and drink that one can imagine' (Letherby and Reynolds 2005, 10). Where else would such a combination of activities have taken place in the 1840s? 'The station was … a gateway through which people passed in endless profusion on a variety of missions … There are countless individual stories encapsulated in the photographs of migrant workers arriving in Continental stations or commuters pouring into the London termini' (Richards and MacKenzie 1986, 7).

Comparison of Rocque's map of London of 1746 (Fig 28) with Stanford's map of 1862 (Fig 29) shows that the future site of Shoreditch station and the later Bishopsgate goods station was in a rapidly urbanising area. Ribbon development had previously been concentrated along Shoreditch High Street, but throughout the late medieval and early post-medieval periods the area between Shoreditch High Street and Brick Lane was infilled with housing, courtyards and factories. To the east of Brick Lane were market gardens and open fields, interspersed with housing. Further development occurred in the area during the century leading up to the construction of the ECR, so that by the 1830s Shoreditch was a crowded settlement on the periphery of the City of London.

The first railway terminus in Shoreditch High Street was shared between the Eastern Counties Railway and the Northern and Eastern Railway Company, which ran services as far as Cambridge. The station had a frontage 125ft (38m) long, and the central pavilion had a street-level basement clad with rusticated stone, and two upper storeys flanked at the northern and southern ends by three-storey corner towers; staircases led from the front of a doorway at basement level up to doors in the sides of the corner towers (Fig 15). A semicircular forecourt was located in front of the sub-basement, and was screened off from Shoredich High Street by the existing row of 17th- to early 19th-century buildings (Fig 7); these were subsequently replaced by the row of single-storey shops visible in Fig 15. Carriage entrances flanked by gas lamps led to the entrance forecourt, and ramps led up to the open canopies abutting the raised ground floor on the northern and southern sides of the station. Pavilions extended eastwards from the corner towers on the northern and southern sides of the train shed, and appear to have had central pediments.

The train shed had single departure and arrival platforms, each over 265ft (80m) long, separated by three carriage sidings (Fig 36; Fig 37). The tracks and platforms were covered by a corrugated wrought iron roof with three pitches, the central pitch having a span of nearly 36ft (11m) and the outer pitches each with a span of 20ft 6in (6.25m). Rainwater drained through 34 cast iron columns which ran in two rows down the length of the shed. The tracks of the departure and arrival platforms and the three central sidings were linked by turntables.

Adjacent to the departure platform were the ticket offices and a horse and carriage dock. Additional horse and carriage docks were located adjacent to the arrival platform, along with a 32ft (9.8m) turntable, engine pit, water crane and coke platform. The railway platforms were at a higher level, above brick vaults which were used for stabling. The upper floors of the station building contained the offices of the ECR and N&ER (Jackson 1985, 108).

The Shoredich terminus changed its name to Bishopsgate station in 1846, perhaps to avoid the connotations of the name 'Shoredich'; the area to the north of the station, especially around Old Nichol Street (Fig 29), was one of the poorest parts of London. Webb Square, which was demolished to make way for the terminus, was described by Rev Timothy Gibson as 'a sort of receptacle for pickpockets, house-breakers and prostitutes, great numbers of whom were removed; and the same along St John Street, one side of which was taken down, and several bad characters were then got rid of' (Royal Commission on Metropolitan Termini, 1846; cited in Jackson 1985, 108).

In 1845 there were already proposals to construct an alternative terminus to that in Shoredich High Street. George Hudson, the chairman of the York and North Midland Railway and, from 1847, of the ECR, spoke of the inconvenience of Shoredich for the City and West End, and supported the idea of a new terminus in Farringdon Street.

In 1847 the viaduct on the approach to the newly renamed Bishopsgate station was widened on its southern side between George Street, on the eastern side of Brick Lane, and the terminus. Various other additions were made to the station as the amount of rail traffic carried by the ECR increased. It has been suggested that the station was partially rebuilt in 1848–9, and that a new frontage was constructed in the Italian style by the architect and engineer Sancton Wood (Jackson 1985, 108). The ECR had received authority in 1846 and 1847 to enlarge the terminus, but no such rebuilding work is mentioned in the accounts, and it appears that the Italianate facade depicted in 1862 (Fig 15) was that of the original terminus building of 1840.

As well as the N&ER, other railway companies shared lines and stations with the ECR, including the London, Tilbury and Southend Railway, established in 1854. With so many East Anglian railway companies dependent on each other, an amalgamation soon took place. Following an Act of Parliament of 7 August 1862, the ECR was grouped with the Eastern Union, East Anglian, East Suffolk and Norfolk Railway Companies to form the Great Eastern Railway (GER Soc website); it was at around this time that Braithwaite's viaduct

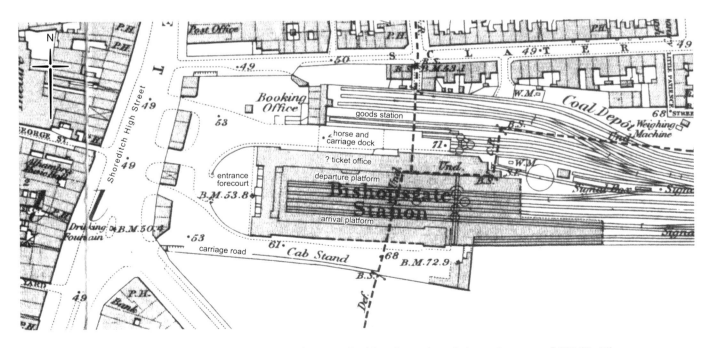

Fig 36 The layout of Shoredich (later Bishopsgate) railway station, shown on a detail from the 1st edition Ordnance Survey map of 1872 (Fig 21)

*Fig 37 The interior of Bishopsgate railway station (*Illustrated London News*, 21 December 1850)*

was widened on its northern side, in order to cope with the traffic from the GER's constituent companies.

4.3 The Braithwaite viaduct: east of Brick Lane

The Eastern Counties Railway was carried through east London into the Shoreditch terminus on a viaduct 1 1/4 miles (2km) in length, often known as the Braithwaite viaduct after the chief engineer of the line. The section of viaduct that was recorded as part of the East London line project had been truncated by the construction of the approach to Liverpool Street station in 1873, so was divided into two parts bisected by the Liverpool Street cutting and Brick Lane (Fig 38). To the east of Brick Lane, in Pedley Street, the viaduct was bounded to the south by

an open yard on the northern side of the later cutting of the East London line of the London Underground, to the east by Fleet Street Hill, and to the north and west by the Liverpool Street cutting. To the west of Brick Lane the viaduct had been incorporated into the later Bishopsgate goods station.

The stretch of Braithwaite's viaduct on the eastern side of Brick Lane, the Pedley Street viaduct (Fig 39), comprised a series of elliptical brick vaults constructed of mixed stock brick. The cross-walls, or piers, of brick laid in English bond supported a projecting impost course of large dressed blocks of fine-grained yellow or grey-yellow sandstone, from which sprang the brick vaulting. The brick vaults consisted of seven concentric courses or 'rings' of stock brick laid in stretcher bond. Each pier was set on a projecting brick plinth, rendered with cement, which itself had stepped foundations of brick. When originally constructed, the arches of the viaduct were open to the street; in the proceedings of the trial at the Old Bailey on 27 February 1843 of George Tappin, who was

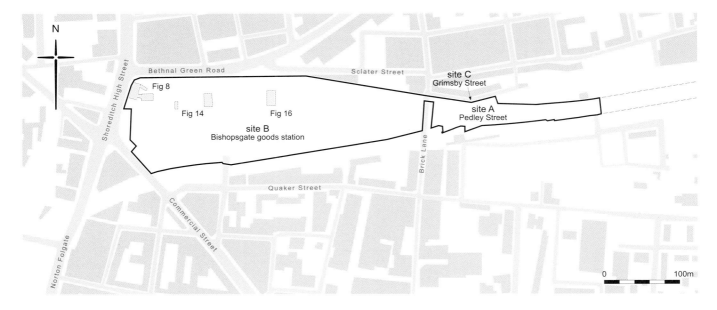

Fig 38 Plan of the sites of Bishopsgate goods station and of the Pedley Street and Grimsby Street viaduct (scale 1:5000)

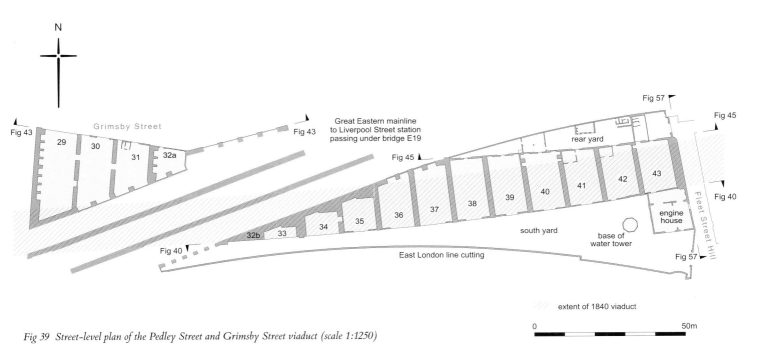

Fig 39 Street-level plan of the Pedley Street and Grimsby Street viaduct (scale 1:1250)

accused of receiving stolen silk weaving-related goods (OB, t18430227-892), Sergeant George Teakle stated that he had observed Tappin and his accomplice James Bryant hiding under a railway arch in St John Street (later renamed Grimsby Street) and was able to apprehend them.

Street directories from the mid 19th century suggest that some of the arches were enclosed at an early date; the Post Office street directory of 1860 (HAD) states that Isaac Gobetz, jeweller, and William Thompson, greengrocer, occupied railway arches adjacent to Brick Lane. At the same time, at the eastern end of St John Street, Richard Garrett and Sons, makers of agricultural implements, occupied an arch close to the ECR's goods station. Richard Garrett and Sons manufactured agricultural equipment and machinery at their factory in Leiston, Suffolk, easily

reached by the ECR; the vacant railway arches enabled them to set up their own warehouse for distributing their products throughout London and internationally.

The arched openings on the southern side of the viaduct (Fig 40; Fig 41), looking on to the open yard on the northern side of the East London line cutting, were largely infilled with brick or cement block walls and a variety of sliding timber or steel plate doors; the doors to arch 37 were fitted to a rail with a mechanism which incorporated a hinge, so that the pair of doors could slide apart or open outwards into the yard. A brick buttress had been incorporated at the time of construction into the fabric of the southern side of the viaduct, on the pier between arches 33 and 34. A photograph showing part of the exterior of the GER horse infirmary in *c* 1911 (Fig 42) indicates that at least some of

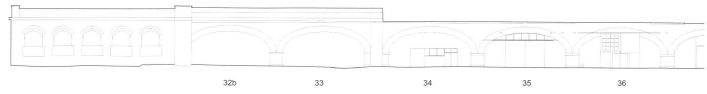

32b	33	34	35	36

Fig 40 The south elevation of the Pedley Street viaduct (scale 1:500)

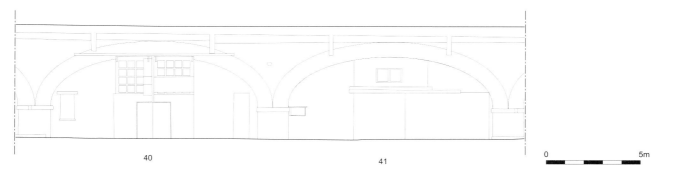

40	41

0   5m

Fig 41 Detail of the south elevation of the Pedley Street viaduct (scale 1:200)

the arches had been infilled on the southern side with rendered or painted brick walls with a low projecting brick plinth. Cast iron-framed windows with small glass panes and stone sills were placed high in the walls, approximately 1.5m above ground level.

A projecting plain cornice of dressed yellow sandstone was positioned above the elliptical brick vaults on the southern side of the viaduct. Where sections of the cornice were missing, perhaps due to bomb damage sustained during the Second World War, they had been rebuilt in brick, and a taller brick parapet wall had been constructed above the cornice towards the western end of the viaduct. The brackets for telegraph wires had been fixed to the parapet wall on the southern side of the viaduct. Telegraphs were used to control the signals for the movement of trains and to transmit messages, and the Regulation Act of 1844 required the railway companies to allow telegraphs to be set up

beside their lines whenever the Board of Trade requested it. The following year, for example, the London and Southampton Railway allowed the erection of a telegraph along its line for the use of the Admiralty, enabling rapid communication between London and Portsmouth. Members of the public were allowed to use this telegraph to send their own messages from railway stations and post offices, and the railway company maintained a separate telegraph line for its own use (Simmons 1995, 75–6).

The southern facade of the western end of the viaduct was truncated by the construction of the Great Eastern mainline to Liverpool Street in the 1870s, resulting in the demolition of the western end, close to Brick Lane, and the construction of a series of parallel walls separating the lines of track, with tall, arched openings. The Great Eastern mainline was constructed on a gradient on the northern side of the viaduct so that it

Fig 42 A railwayman standing outside the Great Eastern Railway's horse infirmary at the Pedley Street viaduct, c 1911 (NRM, SX1114, National Railway Museum/SSPL)

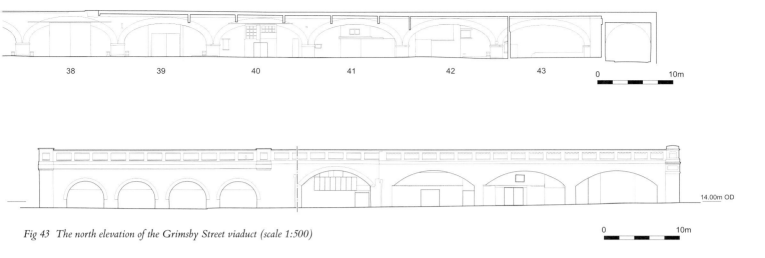

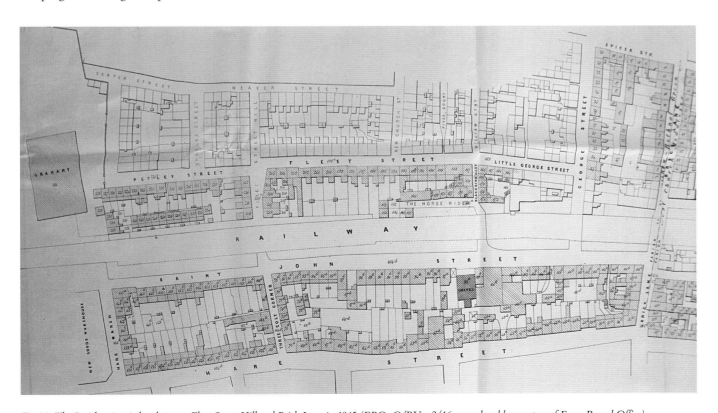

Fig 43   The north elevation of the Grimsby Street viaduct (scale 1:500)

would enter Liverpool Street at a lower level, and cut through the western end of the Pedley Street viaduct, resulting in progressively shorter arches here. The viaduct was rebuilt and widened on its northern side in Grimsby Street (Fig 43), and a bridge, GE19, constructed over the top of the Liverpool Street dive-under to enable trains to still use the viaduct to enter Bishopsgate goods station.

The construction of the Great Eastern mainline also rendered unusable the goods yard in Hare Street on the northern side of the viaduct, and so the Hare Street stables were built on the site in 1881 to house 306 of the GER's horses (Kay 1999, 157–8). The line to Liverpool Street diverged from John Braithwaite's viaduct at Vallance Road, west of Bethnal Green, and progressed along a steep incline so that trains entered

Liverpool Street station below street level.

Several of the arches (34, 35, 36, 37 and 38) showed evidence of having been interconnected via a series of round-headed transverse arches, or cross-vaults. Further arches, closer to Brick Lane, may have incorporated similar transverse arches but were truncated by the construction of the GER mainline in the 1870s. The transverse arches may have facilitated movement between the streets and properties on either side of the viaduct; Blackbird Alley (later abolished) passed through arch 35, and the transverse arches would have allowed access to the adjacent vaults. Further east, on the western side of Fleet Street Hill, the arches appear not to have been connected, although a plan of the viaduct from 1845 (Fig 44) indicates that a lane leading from the western side of Fleet Street Hill served the southern side of

Fig 44   The Braithwaite viaduct between Fleet Street Hill and Brick Lane in 1845 (ERO, Q/RUm 2/46, reproduced by courtesy of Essex Record Office)

arches 40, 41, 42 and 43. Being able to move between the arches and from one side of the viaduct to another unhindered would also have created the kinds of hiding places that George Tappin and James Bryant used during their unsuccessful evasion of the police (above).

In the 1860s the Braithwaite viaduct was widened on its northern side (Fig 45; Fig 46). Thick brick walls added to the northern side of each vault carried a bridge deck of trough-sectioned steel plates; in parts this deck was supported by I-sectioned riveted wrought iron or steel plate girders carried by projecting yellow stock brick piers (Fig 47). The extension was constructed in order to allow a greater number of approach lines into the Bishopsgate passenger terminus in Shoreditch High Street, where a small goods yard had been constructed to the north, and so the extension became progressively wider from east to west.

When the railway viaduct was widened on its northern side,

the opportunity was taken to close the southern and northern end of each arch with a brick wall, which originally incorporated a set of double-leaf doors with overlights and a pair of cast iron-framed windows; the door openings were later partially blocked and single doors installed. The end walls on the southern side of the viaduct were later removed and replaced with walls of concrete blocks, and timber and steel sliding doors. The arches were used as the horse infirmary of the GER; the floors of some of the arches were laid with blue-brick setts, and a central gangway running the length of the arch, from north to south, had open drains to either side, emptying into further open drains in the yard to the north of the viaduct (Fig 48). To either side of the gangway, each arch would have been subdivided into stalls for the horses; these were later removed, but the footings of the posts that divided the stalls marked their former positions, as did the areas of the floor that had been worn by the horses, and the iron tethering

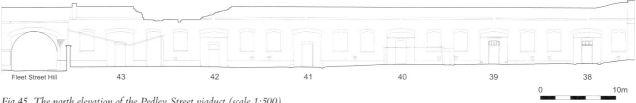

Fleet Street Hill   43   42   41   40   39   38

0   10m

Fig 45 The north elevation of the Pedley Street viaduct (scale 1:500)

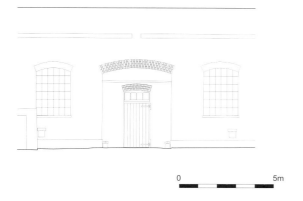

0   5m

Fig 46 Detail of the north elevation of arch 39 of the Pedley Street viaduct (scale 1:200)

Fig 47 Internal view of the extension to the northern side of the Pedley Street viaduct

N

arch 38

arch 41

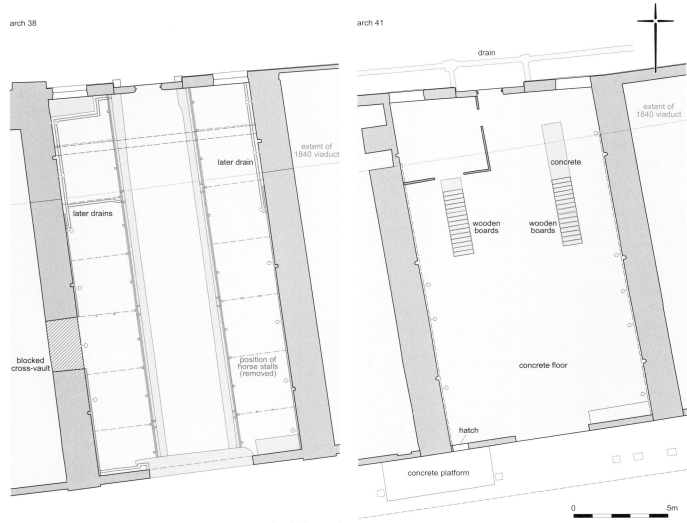

extent of 1840 viaduct

later drain

later drains

blocked
cross-vault

position of
horse stalls
(removed)

drain

extent of
1840 viaduct

concrete

wooden
boards

wooden
boards

concrete floor

hatch

concrete platform

0   5m

Fig 48 Detailed plan of arches 38 and 41 of the Pedley Street viaduct (scale 1:200)

*Fig 49 A tethering
ring and incised arrow
in arch 37 of the
Pedley Street viaduct*

rings fixed to the stone impost course. In some arches, arrows
had been incised into the plaster render below the impost,
perhaps marking where horses with particular injuries should be
kept (Fig 49). The horse infirmary was still operating in the
1930s; a plan of the site (ERO, D/Z 346/3460/49) indicates that
arch 43 was in use as a farrier's workshop, a range of stables
abutted the southern side of the yard in Pedley Street, and a
lean-to shed containing the 'Horse Doctors Office' abutted the
western yard, in the same location as the later concrete water
tower base.

The yard to the north of the Pedley Street viaduct

To the north of the Pedley Street viaduct an open yard was
constructed, paved with granite setts and with a central open
drain into which the drains in each arch emptied. The yard
surface appears to have been laid in two phases; larger granite
setts were laid to the west of arch 40, while those to the east
were much smaller in size. A set of entrance gates with brick
piers at the eastern end of the yard originally opened on to
Fleet Street Hill, before the construction of an extension

abutting the northern side of arch 43. The Pedley Street viaduct was widened on its northern side in the 1860s, and the opportunity was taken to incorporate a set of tall double-leaf doors and a pair of iron-framed windows into the north-facing facade of each arch.

When the Great Eastern mainline approach to Liverpool Street station was constructed, truncating the western end of the viaduct and the yard, the wide entrances on the northern side of each arch would have been rendered largely useless, with little room to turn a cart around in the yard. The wide openings for the double-leaf doors were reduced in size, and single-leaf doors were inserted with iron-framed, stone-silled windows over them (Fig 50).

The brick parapet on the northern side of the viaduct was capped with rounded engineering coping bricks. Below the parapet was a projecting string-course of sandstone blocks which accommodated a break above each arched opening, perhaps for a drainage pipe or gaslight.

Once the construction of the Great Eastern mainline had limited the usefulness of the yard to the north of the viaduct, a number of buildings were constructed within the space. To the north of arch 40 a modern, late 20th-century single-storey building of breeze blocks had been constructed across the door and western window of the northern facade of the arch. A centrally placed pillar, constructed of reused stock bricks, supported a rolled steel joist and the flat timber-framed roof with corrugated iron cladding.

A lean-to structure, probably a stable (Fig 51), was located to the north of arches 42 and 43. The eastern and northern

Fig 50 View of the north elevation of the Pedley Street viaduct, with the Great Eastern mainline cutting wall

Fig 51 The former stable at the eastern end of the yard to the north of the Pedley Street viaduct

walls of this building remained, and it must have been constructed after the Great Eastern mainline since it would have rendered the entrance gates from Fleet Street Hill to the east useless, although pedestrians and horses would still have been able to pass it to the north; the space between the stable and the cutting wall of the Great Eastern mainline was not infilled until later in the 20th century. The eastern wall of the structure had a series of tethering rings, suggesting that it had been used as a stable. The scars of a single pitched roof were visible in the north-facing external wall of arch 42, which would have formed the southern wall of the stable, and in the northern wall which projected out into the yard.

To the north of arch 41, abutting the Great Eastern mainline cutting wall, was a single-storey structure of brick laid in English bond with a flat roof of corrugated iron sheeting. The cutting wall formed the rear (northern) wall of the building. The structure contained a single room, heated by a fireplace in a projecting chimney-breast in the western wall of the building. The building was entered by a door at the eastern end of the southern wall, and three segmental-arched windows were also positioned in the southern wall. A single segmental-arched window was placed in the centre of the eastern wall. The structure appears to have been built some time between 1916, when the 3rd edition Ordnance Survey map of the area was produced, and 1961, when the building is shown on a revised large-scale Ordnance Survey map. On stylistic grounds, it is suggested that the structure was built as a shelter or office for the workers at the horse infirmary in the 1920s or 1930s.

The Great Eastern mainline cutting wall was constructed in the early 1870s, when the approach to Liverpool Street station was built. The wall was constructed of mixed stock brick laid in English bond and was capped with rounded blue engineering coping bricks. Refuge recesses for railway company personnel were later inserted into the wall; the Great Eastern mainline was built at a level only slightly lower than that of the yard to the north of the viaduct, so that when the refuges were built they had to project above the yard surface. The refuges were constructed of red machine-made brick, with a concrete slab roof.

The northern wall of arch 34 of the Pedley Street viaduct indicates how the northern side of the viaduct was truncated by the construction of the Liverpool Street cutting. The northern walls of arches 33, 34 and 35 incorporated a 'dog-leg', or kink, shown on the ground-level plan of the bridge GE19 site. The eastern half of the northern wall was positioned at a right angle to the eastern internal wall of each arch. The western half of the northern wall formed the southern side of the Liverpool Street cutting wall, and the two differently orientated walls were joined by a short stretch of brick wall. This necessitated the inclusion of a void within the northern wall of each arch, which was visible during the demolition of the structure. This reduced the number of bricks required for construction, in turn reducing the weight of the structure and limiting the need for more substantial foundations.

Arches 33, 34, 35, 36 and 37 had been truncated by the construction of the Great Eastern mainline, and as a result were

increasingly shorter in depth towards the western end of the viaduct. To the immediate west of arch 33 was a blind arch; the southern facade of the structure had been retained, but with no vault behind it, and the arch was infilled with brick. Arches 36 and 37 both had a pair of arched iron-framed glazed windows in tall arched recesses in the northern wall, facing on to the Great Eastern mainline.

Cast iron 'weepers' were inserted into the fabric of the brick piers between the arches; vertical channels were cut into the brick, and cast iron drainpipes were inserted to drain rainwater from the track level of the viaduct into drains running from north to south. The drainpipes were then covered with render to conceal them.

Several of the arches contained rendered brick-built open-topped structures abutting the northern and southern end walls. The walls above these structures were often blackened with soot, and it is suggested that the structures contained coppers for heating water, or small hearths for the farriers who worked in the GER's horse infirmary, which occupied the arches in the late 19th and early 20th centuries.

The water-softening plant

The parapet wall of the viaduct had been truncated by an extension to its southern side, which formerly carried a siding. This was constructed of reinforced concrete, cast *in situ*, and formed part of a group of structures which also included the base of a water tower (Fig 52) and a 'sludge house', which was built to contain the sludge press of a water-softening plant (Fig 53). The operation of the railways required huge quantities of water, but the hard water in the south-east was unsuitable for use in the boilers of steam locomotives, as a residue would form inside the boiler, reducing its efficiency, in the same way as limescale forms on the heating element of a kettle or washing machine, albeit on a much larger scale. The sludge press extracted the solid matter present in untreated water, resulting in purified water suitable for use in steam locomotive boilers.

A plan of the proposed new water-softening plant from December 1934 (not illustrated) indicates that a timber gantry for a railway siding had been located in the same position as the later concrete structure, which was extended over Fleet Street Hill. The concrete siding structure was supported by a series of reinforced concrete struts which had supplementary diagonal bracing towards the eastern end, where it had to support the additional weight of the sludge house. A cut had been made in the south-facing facade of the viaduct in the pier between arches 42 and 43 to accommodate a reinforced concrete beam supporting the former railway siding.

The reinforced concrete base of the water tower originally supported a tall water tank (Fig 54). The tank was probably removed when the adjacent Brick Lane goods depot was closed between 1964 and 1967; in any case, the water-softening plant would not have been required after the introduction of electrically powered trains. The concrete slab water tower base was supported by two concentric sets of reinforced concrete

Fig 52 The reinforced cast concrete base of the water tower of the water-softening plant, looking north-east

Fig 53 The sludge house on the upper level of the viaduct, looking east

vertical struts: an inner set of four struts and an outer set of eight struts. Each outer strut was connected to an inner strut by a diagonal brace of reinforced concrete, and the whole structure had been cast *in situ*. At ground level, contained within the inner struts, was a cast concrete tank, diagonal in plan. Circular apertures in the water tower's platform would have allowed pipes to connect the large water tank above to the lower concrete tank, which had a projecting ledge, perhaps for resting a ladder, and painted 'Mind Your Head' notices had been stencilled on the concrete beam above. Immediately to the west of the water tower, an underground tank was covered with timber planks.

Fig 54 The Spitalfields water-softening plant in 1937, looking south-east (NRM, SX1821, National Railway Museum/SSPL)

The most prominent structure on the top of the viaduct was the housing for the sludge press. The sludge house was rectangular in plan and had a reinforced concrete frame structure, cast *in situ*; the spaces between the vertical concrete posts were filled with concrete panels, and windows were positioned in the northern, southern and western elevations. The concrete panels on the southern and western sides of the structure had been painted white. A door opening was positioned in the western elevation, and a projecting concrete platform would have allowed staff to gain entry to the sludge house via a ladder. The corrugated iron roof, part of which had been removed from the structure, was supported by the gable ends of the sludge house and by three steel trusses, supported by the vertical concrete posts in the northern and southern elevations of the structure.

The sludge house originally contained a press which extracted impurities from the water (Fig 55). Internally, the sludge house was divided into two rooms by a partition wall, creating a small room at the eastern end of the structure. The floor of the larger room had a void, covered with timber boards, which may originally have been a trapdoor. The sludge house was supported on four tall reinforced concrete legs; its underside was blackened with soot, suggesting that steam locomotives would draw up beneath the structure to have their boilers filled with purified water.

The upper track level

The upper track level of the Pedley Street viaduct (Fig 56) was covered with gravel and scrub at the time of the survey; it had been left largely disused since the closure of Bishopsgate goods station after the fire in December 1964. The railway tracks, points and signals were lifted, and the remaining structures went out of use.

A number of structures were concentrated on the upper level of bridge GE19. These included the concrete footing for

Fig 55 The interior of the Spitalfields sludge house in 1937 (NRM, SX1822, National Railway Museum/SSPL)

an overhead gantry or signal, three open-topped concrete silos, which may have held chemicals for use in the water-softening plant, a timber shed and a brick lavatory block, and an air-raid shelter. The shelter was designed to stand above ground, rather than being buried below the ground like an Anderson shelter. It

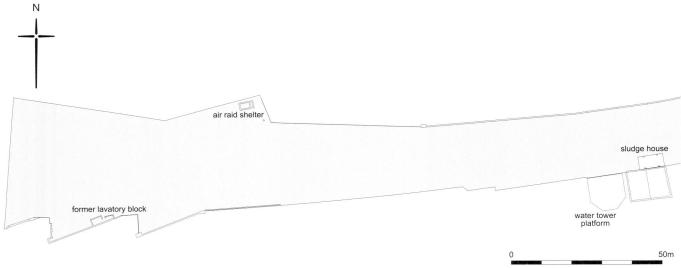

N

Fig 56 Plan of the upper track level of the Pedley Street viaduct (scale 1:1250)

was rectangular in plan and constructed of machine-made bricks laid in English bond; the walls were 0.34m thick, the equivalent of three bricks in thickness. The shelter had a blast-proof entrance and an escape hatch in the concrete slab roof. It may have been used by the drivers of goods trains who found themselves stranded on the viaduct during an air raid, with no opportunity to reach the relative safety of ground level. London's railway infrastructure was a key target for aerial bombardment during the Second World War, and the Pedley Street viaduct shows some evidence of blast damage sustained during the Blitz.

The engine house

An engine house, located on the southern side of arch 43, adjacent to Fleet Street Hill, provided power for the cranes used to move goods in the granaries of the Brick Lane (later Spitalfields) goods depot on the eastern side of Fleet Street Hill. The engine house was constructed shortly after the viaduct, and was standing by 1848. It was built of yellow stock brick laid in English bond, and was stylistically similar to the granary buildings of the Brick Lane goods depot, where the tons of grain required by the expanding population of London were brought in by train from the fields of East Anglia (Fig 57). The opening of Bishopsgate goods station had taken some of the trade away from the Brick Lane depot, and so the granary buildings had already gone into something of a decline by the time they were burnt down in 1919. The goods depot carried on, but finally closed in 1967 and was largely demolished in that year, with the exception of part of the granary on the eastern side of Fleet Street Hill, and the engine house (Kay 1999, 161–2).

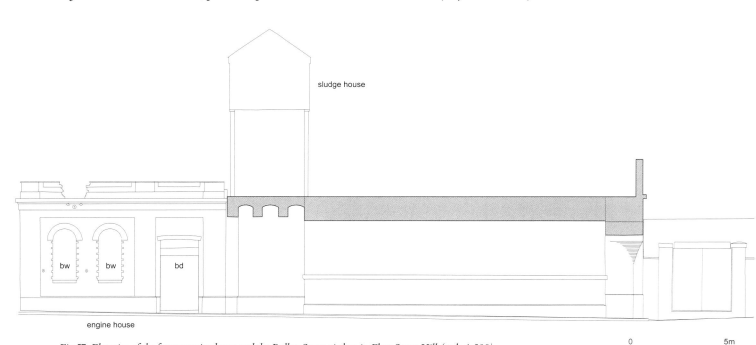

Fig 57 Elevation of the former engine house and the Pedley Street viaduct in Fleet Street Hill (scale 1:200)

The eastern and western walls of the engine house had tall round-headed arched windows with yellow sandstone sills, and there was a tall, wide, low segmental-arched door opening on the eastern side of the building (Fig 58). The southern wall of the building was significantly altered during the 20th century, when it was demolished and rebuilt, perhaps when the engine, boiler and other machinery were removed; the earlier hipped pitched roof, with a louvered lantern and projecting plain sandstone cornice below the roofline, was replaced by a steel truss roof.

The engine would have required a boiler house with a chimney and fuel store; there was no evidence for such structures on the site, although these may have been housed in part within the railway arches of the viaduct, and removed when the water-softening plant was constructed on the site in the 1930s. Coal to fuel the engine may have been delivered to the engine house via the sidings at viaduct level.

Inside the engine house, all evidence for the building's former use had been removed and the walls whitewashed, obscuring any scars caused by flywheels and other moving machinery, and there were no apertures for belts or line shafts to transmit power to the granaries in the eastern wall of the engine house.

Most of the granaries of the Brick Lane goods depot were badly damaged by fire in 1919, and were demolished shortly afterwards (Kay 1999, 158). Part of the 'second granary', which stood on the eastern side of Fleet Street Hill, remained

standing; it was stylistically similar to the engine house, being constructed of yellow stock brick laid in English bond, and stood on a projecting brick plinth. The tall round-headed arched windows had yellow sandstone sills, and projecting brick pilasters provided additional reinforcement for the external walls. The granary was taller than the viaduct, as it was served by internal sidings at viaduct level.

4.4 West of Brick Lane: the approach to Shoreditch station

At the time of its construction, the Eastern Counties Railway was carried over Brick Lane by a brick-built elliptical arched bridge, similar to the arches of the viaduct. In 1842 the Crown brought a case against the ECR, as they had failed to incorporate sufficient clearance for vehicles below the arch. The height from the surface of the road to the centre of the arch was less than the required minimum of 16ft (4.9m), so the company was allowed to lower the level of the street under the arch (Carrow and Oliver 1846, 22–33). The arched bridge had a relatively short life, and was replaced by a wrought iron bridge when the dive-under to Liverpool Street station was constructed, cutting the viaduct in two.

Like the viaduct on the eastern side of Brick Lane, the Braithwaite viaduct on the approach to Shoreditch station was constructed of mixed stock brick and comprised a series of broad elliptical vaults. Later truncation during the construction of Bishopsgate goods station reduced the length of this stretch of the viaduct to 20 arches. The piers were pierced by one, two or three pointed cross-vaults, dressed with yellow stock brick, which allowed communication and pedestrian access between the vaults but were not sufficiently wide for vehicles to pass through (Fig 59). The use of pointed arches for the cross-vaults, rather than the round-headed arches seen on the eastern side of Brick Lane, may have been for aesthetic reasons, as they were associated with the railway line's terminus.

The piers, with bricks laid in English bond, stood on projecting plinths which had been rendered in many of the vaults and where the viaduct crossed Wheler Street. The vaulting, which comprised seven rings of bricks laid in stretcher bond, sprang from the projecting stone impost band. Many of the vaults contained circular apertures at the apex, which may have been intended to ventilate each vault and its contents. Such apertures were not apparent in the vaults which were originally constructed to accommodate Farthing Street or Vine Street, nor in any of the arches to the east of Brick Lane, which were left open to the street when they were originally constructed.

The Braithwaite viaduct continued over Wheler Street, and the fragmentary and irregular nature of the early fabric on the western side of the street may indicate the easternmost extent of the original terminus. Openings for a door and two

Fig 58 The former engine house in Fleet Street Hill

Fig 59 A pointed cross-vault connecting two of the arches of the Braithwaite viaduct on the western side of Brick Lane, looking east

4.5 The construction and development of Bishopsgate goods station

Despite measures to increase the capacity of Shoreditch (later Bishopsgate) station, by the mid 1860s the terminus had reached its full capacity. In December 1862, a report to the board of the newly formed Great Eastern Railway recommended once again that a new passenger terminus should be constructed within the City of London, allowing for the construction of additional lines to develop suburban services, and that the old terminus be converted to a goods station. The old Bishopsgate station was 'objectionable in almost every feature. In locality it is remote; its approaches are inconvenient; and as regards space, it is so restricted that your traffic can only be carried at great cost, with great delay, and with an absolute restriction on the number of trains which can be despatched' (cited in Jackson 1985, 109).

In 1865, Parliamentary authority was granted to replace Bishopsgate station, and an alternative passenger terminus was constructed at Liverpool Street. The transfer of the GER's London terminus from Bishopsgate to the much larger site in Liverpool Street, within the boundary of the City of London, reflected the increasing amount of traffic that the railways were carrying. The construction of a dedicated goods station allowed fresh produce from rural East Anglia, and Continental imports arriving via the port of Harwich, to be distributed to warehouses and markets across east London.

The 1st edition Ordnance Survey map of 1872 (Fig 21) shows Bishopsgate station and the coal depot which had been constructed to the north, and the areas to the south of the station that were cleared of housing in preparation for the construction of the approach to Liverpool Street station. Following the opening of that station in 1874, Bishopsgate station closed in November 1875. An order was made in December 1876 for the plans for the conversion into a goods station to be prepared; this work was carried out by the GER's engineer, Alfred A Langley. Demolition and reconstruction were carried out between 1878 and 1880, and the new goods station, covering an area of 11 acres (4.45ha), opened in January 1881 (Fig 60). A visit to the goods station during the final phase of construction by members of the Society of Engineers was recorded in the Society's journal (Anon 1881). The goods station was built by Messrs Vernon and Ewens of Cheltenham, and had three storeys: the street-level basement, the viaduct-level platforms and tracks of the goods station, and the warehouse, all supported above the platforms by a series of cast iron columns and wrought iron girders; the iron and glass roof of the warehouse was supported by lattice girders, which in turn rested on further iron columns. The construction of Bishopsgate goods station removed much of the first rail terminus built by the Eastern Counties Railway. Only the Braithwaite viaduct and the eastern wall of the street-level basement of the station were retained and incorporated into the new structure, even though the Society of Engineers commented on the substantial nature of the previous building, constructed using 'Roman' cement.

elongated windows were located in the western pier of the bridge spanning Wheler Street, and would have served the eastern end of the basement of the Shoreditch passenger terminus.

In 1847 the Braithwaite viaduct to the west of Brick Lane was widened on its southern side in order to carry additional lines into the station. The southern side of the existing viaduct was cut back to allow the extension to be block-bonded into the existing fabric, and the upper parts of the earlier viaduct were remodelled. The later extension was constructed in red brick, with the piers standing on projecting plinths, and the brick vaulting sprang from a projecting brick impost. The brick courses of the piers and vaulting were laid in English bond, and the profile of the vaulting was a taller, less pronounced ellipse than that of the earlier part of the Braithwaite viaduct. The viaduct was widened on its northern side in the 1860s, like the equivalent stretch on the eastern side of Brick Lane, in order to carry the increasing quantity of rail traffic that the passenger terminus and its goods depot attracted; this later addition does not survive, however, as it was demolished when the Braithwaite viaduct was enveloped in the new vaults of Bishopsgate goods station.

The northern and southern elevations of the goods station were evenly divided into bays with gable ends, by rusticated pilasters of white brick rising from the blue engineering brick piers of the street-level basement vaults. The red brick facade of each bay contained two tiers of three grouped windows, dressed with white brick, the lower windows having segmental-arched heads whereas the upper windows had round-arched heads. The upper storey was divided from those below by a cornice, and each gable featured a small round window (Fig 61). A later two-storey addition of irregular plan almost concealed the original front from view. The lower part of this front was open, and massive piers of blue engineering brick, 5ft (1.52m) square, supported the girders carrying the front of the offices in the upper storey. This was of dark red brick, and in the centre and at each end was a projecting bay containing a group of four round-headed windows. Between the bays were two ranges of nine windows with segmental-arched heads; all the windows were dressed with white brick and moulded terracotta (Sheppard 1957, 255).

Across the front of the goods station extended a bracketed entablature of terracotta (Fig 62). The frieze contained moulded or carved lettering spelling 'Bishopsgate Goods Station', with a circular rosette and garlands above, the rosette containing the badge of the Great Eastern Railway Company which incorporated the shields of the principal towns and cities served by the railway company. The additions to the front of the goods station had simple elevations of red brick, divided into bays by rusticated pilasters of white brick. Each bay contained a pair of round-headed windows and was finished with a corbel below the parapet (Sheppard 1957, 255). Inside the goods station, the offices and porters' mess room and canteen were located at the front of the building, mainly on the upper floors which were destroyed by fire in December 1964.

While the railway line to Liverpool Street station was under construction, platforms were provided in the cutting below the southern side of Bishopsgate station. These opened for use in November 1872 and served for two years as a temporary terminus for some trains until the railway lines could be extended to the new Liverpool Street station. The station was known initially as Bishopsgate low-level station, and had two platforms below the western side of Wheler Street and one below the eastern side. The booking office could be reached from entrances in Commercial Street and Shoreditch High Street. Two additional platforms were constructed and opened in 1891, along with a new entrance in one of the viaduct arches facing Commercial Street. The low-level station was closed on 22 May 1916 as a wartime economy measure, but was never re-opened (Connor 2000, 43).

In 1882 the vaults to the east of Wheler Street opened as wholesale food markets (Guillery 1995, 2), the arches to the north of the central roadway being used for fish and those to the south for potatoes (Anon 1881). The trustees of Spitalfields market saw the GER's new market as a threat to their own business, and secured a court injunction obliging the traders to leave. Retail businesses were transferred to Columbia market in Bethnal Green, although many traders retained their arches for

warehousing (Connor 2000, 40).

Initially hoists powered by gas engines were used to raise and lower wagons from one level of the goods station to another (Anon 1881) but these were soon replaced by hydraulic power. Two hydraulic accumulators (Fig 63) were installed in the 1890s in chambers to the south of the western end of the southern roadway ('London Road' on Fig 60). Corresponding chambers on the western side of Wheler Street formerly contained the steam engines, coal stores and fitting shops.

The GER ceased to exist on 31 December 1922. The various railway companies across the country were grouped together to become the 'Big Four', namely the Great Western Railway, the London, Midland and Scottish Railway, the Southern Railway, and the London and North Eastern Railway; it was this last railway company which swallowed up the GER, along with several other companies, most notably the Great Northern Railway Company which ran services from King's Cross station (Connor 2000, 15).

As the 20th century progressed, the amount of freight being carried by the railways began to decline, and in the post-Second World War period the increasing volume of goods being carried by lorries on the new motorway network sealed the fate of many rail goods yards and stations. Perhaps surprisingly, the volume of goods being received at Bishopsgate was increasing, as the goods station handled traffic from recently closed goods yards in the Lea valley (Morgan 1965, 80). On 5 December 1964 a fire broke out in the buildings adjoining the tracks at the western end of Bishopsgate goods station, destroying much of the structure above the viaduct level (ibid) and killing two duty Customs officials, George Humphrey and Thomas Tanner (Anon 1964). Over the following months the buildings on the site were demolished, with the exception of the street-level basement vaults; the costs and complexities of clearing the site and preparing it for construction, when it lay so close to an operational rail line, were at the time so prohibitive that the goods station site was never redeveloped (Nabarro and Richards 1980, 92). The site was subsequently used as a car park and a car-breaker's yard, and later had a go-carting arena installed on the upper level, with a weekend market operating under the arches of the Braithwaite viaduct (Subterranea Brit website).

4.6   The survey: Bishopsgate goods station

The exterior of Bishopsgate goods station

The surviving parts of Bishopsgate goods station were constructed largely of red stock brick and blue engineering brick, with white brick and stone dressings, especially on the panelled parapet walls above the ground-floor level of the goods station and wrapping around its northern side in Bethnal Green Road, forming the parapet of the Brick Lane railway bridge and the viaduct in Grimsby Street. The main vehicle and pedestrian entrance to Bishopsgate goods station (Fig 64)

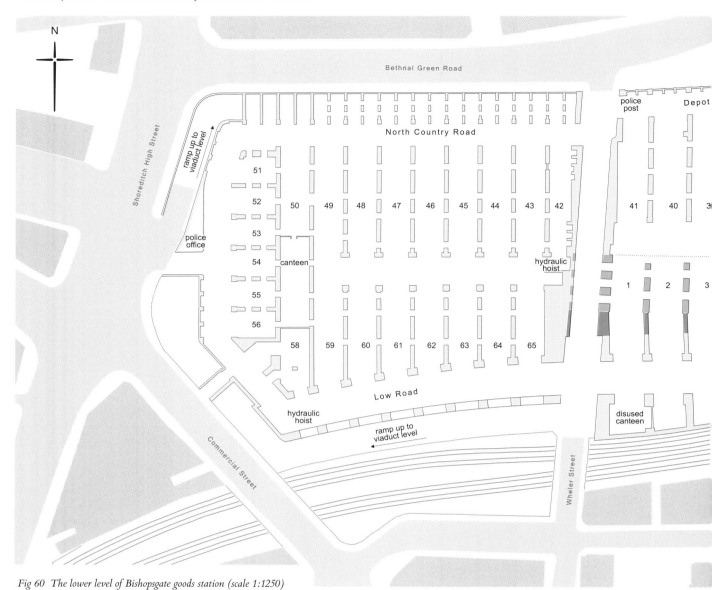

N

Bethnal Green Road

ramp up to viaduct level

North Country Road

police post

Depot

Shoredsitch High Street

51

52

50   49   48   47   46   45   44   43   42

41   40   3

police office

53

54   canteen

hydraulic hoist

55

1   2   3

56

58   59   60   61   62   63   64   65

Low Road

hydraulic hoist

ramp up to viaduct level

Commercial Street

Wheler Street

disused canteen

Fig 60 The lower level of Bishopsgate goods station (scale 1:1250)

Fig 61 The southern side of Bishopsgate goods station in 1955 (City of London, London Metropolitan Archives, SC/PHL/02/629)

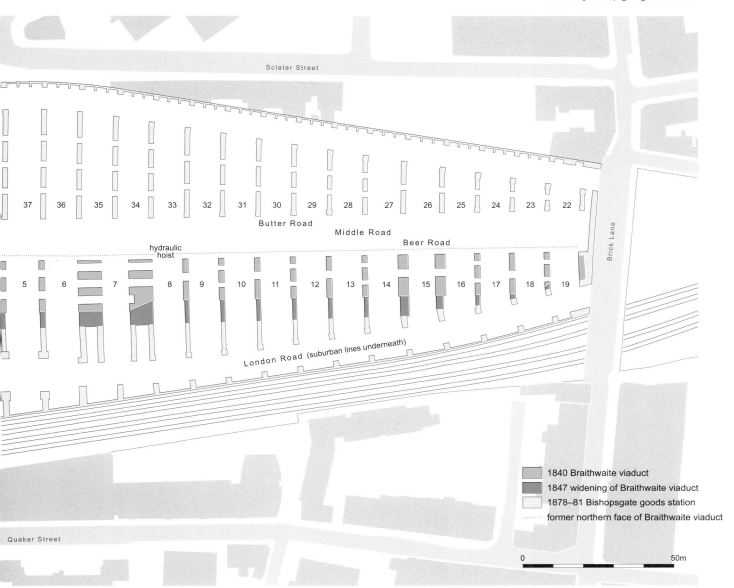

Sclater Street

37 36 35 34 33 32 31 30 29 28 27 26 25 24 23 22

Brick Lane

Butter Road

Middle Road

Beer Road

hydraulic
hoist

5 6 7 8 9 10 11 12 13 14 15 16 17 18 19

London Road (suburban lines underneath)

1840 Braithwaite viaduct
1847 widening of Braithwaite viaduct
1878–81 Bishopsgate goods station
former northern face of Braithwaite viaduct

Quaker Street

0   50m

*Fig 62 The main entrance
to Bishopsgate goods station
in 1962, looking east (City
of London, London
Metropolitan Archives,
SC/PHL/02/626)*

Fig 63 A hydraulic accumulator at Bishopsgate goods station

was situated in Shoreditch High Street, one of the main thoroughfares leading north from the City, so it was here that the decorative embellishments to the structure were concentrated. The remaining part of the main facade in Shoreditch High Street was constructed of blue brick, laid in English bond, and incorporated a series of arched vaults which formerly accommodated retail premises. Above the ground floor was a white brick parapet wall with recessed red brick panels and a dentil course, with white brick dressings and stone copings.

The main entrance originally featured a pair of wrought iron entrance gates, which led from Shoreditch High Street to the street-level transit area inside the goods station. Each gate comprised three panels with a large ornamental medallion in the central panel. Above the entrance gates was a carved stone lintel with scrolled details, supported by wrought iron brackets with scrolled medallions, similar to those on the gates below. The lintel appears to have borne lettering spelling 'Great Eastern Railway', although this had been removed by 1966, probably

after the GER merged with a number of other railway companies in 1923 to become the London and North Eastern Railway Company (above, 4.5). Above the stone lintel was a three-light stone oriel window with relief panels, cornice and columns. The window screened the weighing office outside the main road entrance to the viaduct-level goods station, which was demolished after being severely damaged in the fire of December 1964.

A ramped roadway to the north of the main entrance would have carried vehicles to and from the upper level of the goods station. The outer wall of the north ramp, which wrapped around the corner of Shoreditch High Street and Bethnal Green Road, was constructed of red brick with Bramley Fall stone coping; the lower part of the wall was constructed of blue engineering brick. The area below the ramped roadway contained a number of arched vaults which opened on to Bethnal Green Road and were let out as shops. The wall formed the northern wall of the street-level vaults and the northern boundary of the goods station, and continued round into

Fig 64 The main entrance to Bishopsgate goods station for vehicles and pedestrians in Shoreditch High Street, looking south-east

Bethnal Green Road and Sclater Street.

At the entrance to the ramped northern roadway stood a long, single gate of four panels with medallions, similar to the pair of gates at the main entrance to the goods station (above). The gate was fixed to an ornamental cast iron pier, which doubled as a gaslight standard, at the southern side of the entrance to the ramped roadway. When closed, the gate fastened to a shorter pier which was attached to the wall of the goods station, to the east. The two piers featured relief rosettes, similar to the medallions on the gates, and a shield featuring the cross of St George, which formed the centre of the Great Eastern Railway Company's shield. The piers and gates were manufactured by Barnard Bishop and Barnards, of London and Norwich, in 1884 (Guillery 1995, 3).

A bridge carried the upper level of the goods station over Wheler Street, a road which pre-dated the construction of the Eastern Counties Railway, and formed the boundary between the parishes of St Leonard Shoreditch and St Mary Spital. The red brick piers of the Wheler Street bridge, decorated with white brick dressings, stone cornices and coping, supported riveted wrought iron plate composite beams with intermediate brick jack-arches; the northernmost beam, visible from Bethnal Green Road, was supported by ornate cast iron brackets, similar to those above the main entrance in Shoreditch High Street. To the east of Wheler Street, the northern wall of the goods station curved towards the south, as the number of tracks carrying traffic to and from the goods station was reduced, and the street-level vaults were shortened in length. Instead of containing broad arched vaults which opened on to the street, the eastern end of the northern facade contained a series of recessed arches (Fig 65), each containing an arched window opening with a cast iron window frame with rosettes at the intersections of the glazing bars, stone sills and white brick dressings (Fig 66).

Fig 65 The northern facade of Bishopsgate goods station in Sclater Street, looking south-east

Fig 66 *A window opening in the northern facade of Bishopsgate goods station in Sclater Street*

The eastern boundary of Bishopsgate goods station was located on the western side of Brick Lane, and was marked on its north-eastern corner by the pier of the bridge which carried the railway lines over Brick Lane and on to the Grimsby Street and Pedley Street viaduct (Fig 67). The internal roadways that ran along the northern and southern sides of the goods station opened out on to Brick Lane, providing alternative access to the internal vaults and the market and storage facilities which they contained.

Bishopsgate goods station was bounded to the south by the mainline into Liverpool Street station. To the east of Wheler Street, the southern boundary wall of the goods station was largely open-sided, with blue brick piers carrying the viaduct-level lines and street-level southern internal roadway on riveted wrought iron plate beams with intermediate brick jack-arches (Fig 68). Further railway lines, carrying suburban train services into Liverpool Street station, passed below the southern internal roadway. To the immediate east of the bridge carrying Wheler Street over the Liverpool Street mainline, a number of double-height vaults were accommodated in the space between the mainline and suburban line. These were open on the northern side and could be accessed from the southern internal roadway; within the southern facade each vault contained three tall, arched windows. One of the vaults contained the remains of a hydraulic accumulator which provided the goods station's two wagon hoists and numerous lifts with power (Fig 63). A ramped roadway, similar to that on the northern side of the goods station, ran up to the viaduct level from the western side of Wheler Street. The area beneath the roadway was occupied by

Fig 67 *The Brick Lane bridge, looking south*

Fig 68 London Road, the internal roadway on the southern side of Bishopsgate goods station, looking west

several arched vaults, a number of which had formerly accommodated the street entrance to the platforms on either side of the suburban railway lines.

The interior of Bishopsgate goods station, east of Wheler Street

The goods station structure on the eastern side of Wheler Street was broadly similar to that on the western side, and was dictated in part by the alignment of the vaults in the Braithwaite viaduct to the south. An internal covered roadway (Depot Road), illuminated on its northern side by arched window openings looking on to Bethnal Green Road and Sclater Street, connected Wheler Street and Brick Lane (Fig 69). Historic plans of the goods station indicate the presence of weighbridges at the eastern and western end of the roadway. Arched vaults of red brick were constructed to the south of the roadway (Fig 70). The arched vaults had a span of approximately 40ft (12.2m) from the centre of each pier to the next, so that they were aligned with the arches of the Braithwaite viaduct to the south, and round-headed transverse arches, or cross-vaults, allowed communication between the vaults (Fig 71). The floors of the vaults were raised to incorporate a semi-basement; the concrete floors were supported by wrought iron beams carried by a central spine wall. The western six arches were of the same length, but those to the east were progressively shorter, as the railway lines on the viaduct level above merged together to take traffic away from the goods station.

At the time of a previous survey, carried out by the Royal Commission on Historical Monuments of England (Guillery 1995), a former wagon repair shop was located at the eastern end of the arches and still had what appeared to be its original timber roof. A narrow vaulted passage between the northern and central covered roadways was accommodated at the eastern end of the arches. This had been blocked at its southern end and a door opening constructed at the northern end so that it could serve as an office, perhaps for the wagon repair shop or to monitor the weighbridge adjacent to the Brick Lane entrance.

The arched vaults were separated from the Braithwaite viaduct to the south by a central covered roadway (Fig 72), with paired wrought iron girder and brick jack-arch roofing spanning 46ft (14m) and originally containing three lines of rails. These railway lines were on a different alignment from those to the west of Wheler Street, meaning that it was not possible to transport wagons between the two halves of the street-level goods station. A hydraulic wagon hoist, which carried trucks down from the sidings outside the main viaduct-level warehouse, was located over the centre of the central railway line.

Historic plans of the goods station indicate that the northern set of rails served a continuous platform along the southern side of the northern vaults, and a series of wagon turntables located along the southern set of rails served sidings located in nine of the eastern Braithwaite viaduct arches to the south of the covered roadway. At the time of the RCHME

Fig 69 Depot Road, on the northern side of Bishopsgate goods station, looking west

Fig 70 An arched vault on the southern side of Depot Road, looking north

survey in the early 1990s (Guillery 1995), parts of the turntables were still *in situ*; they were 15ft (4.57m) in diameter and of girder-frame construction with wrought iron tensioning rods. Also at that time, the nine arches with sidings had semi-basements under raised timber floors and check-in booths in their south-west corners (ibid, 5); they may have been constructed as part of the fitting of market offices in the street-level goods station by Bangs and Company in 1881–2.

Fig 71 Cross-vaults connecting the arches on the southern side of Depot Road, looking west

Fig 72 The central internal roadway of Bishopsgate goods station, looking west

The central covered roadway

The central covered roadway was connected, via turntables and two short railway lines at the centre and western end of the Braithwaite viaduct, to the covered roadway on the southern side of the viaduct, 'London Road' (Fig 68), which, like the other covered railways and roadways in the street-level goods station, was roofed with wrought iron girders and intermediate brick jack-arches. This southern covered roadway was located over the low-level suburban railway line into

59

Liverpool Street station. A single railway line ran along the southern covered roadway between Wheler Street and Brick Lane, and historic plans indicate that, as with the northern roadway, there was a weighbridge located at either end of the southern roadway to monitor the movement of goods around Bishopsgate goods station.

The interior of Bishopsgate goods station, west of Wheler Street

The western section of the street-level part of Bishopsgate goods station had its main entrance in Shoreditch High Street, which led to a covered roadway running from north to south at the western end of the goods station. This served vaulted storage areas to the east and west; those on the western side opened out on to Shoreditch High Street and had been in use as shops until the redevelopment of the site began, with some of the smaller arches used as offices. Arched brick vaults on the eastern side of the western roadway had latterly been used as a canteen and kitchen. At the southern end of the western roadway were staircases (Fig 73) leading down to a mid-level landing, from which a further staircase led to a brick-lined tunnel (Fig 74) which emerged on the northern side of the suburban line into Liverpool Street. Historic plans of the goods station indicate that a footbridge formerly led from the mid-level landing to the southern side of these lines, and to the vaults between the suburban and mainline railways.

Covered roadways, spanned by riveted wrought iron plate beams with intermediate brick jack-arches, extended along the northern and southern sides of the interior of the street-level part of Bishopsgate goods station, from the western covered roadway as far as Wheler Street, and small arched vaults opened off the northern side of the northern covered roadway. These arches opened on to Bethnal Green Road and had been used as shops, and were interconnected by a series of cross-vaults. It is likely that the arches were used as offices, mess rooms and for small-scale storage, as they were not connected by railway lines to other parts of the goods station.

A covered railway, also spanned by riveted wrought iron plate beams and brick jack-arches, bisected the central vaults between the northern and southern covered roadways. An opening in the ceiling of the vaults, for a wagon hoist, was located at the eastern end of the railway, adjacent to Wheler Street but separated from it by the western wall of Wheler Street; this allowed wagons containing goods to be brought down from the railway lines on the viaduct above. A double line of tracks, the northernmost having seven wagon turntables, served sidings which extended into each of the arched vaults to the north; each vault was constructed with one narrow and one broad platform. A further siding extended southwards from the western end of the central railway; historic plans of the goods station indicate that this would have extended southwards to a wagon turntable at the western end of the southern covered roadway, from which a further set of tracks ran east, terminating before the junction of Wheler Street, and west to a wagon hoist.

Fig 73 The stairs from the street entrance of Bishopsgate goods station to Bishopsgate low-level passenger station

Fig 74 The pedestrian subway leading to Bishopsgate low-level passenger station, looking west

The viaduct level of Bishopsgate goods station

The warehouses and platforms of Bishopsgate goods station were demolished after being badly damaged by fire in December 1964. The inclined roadway on the northern side of the goods station was paved with granite setts, and a line of setts laid end-to-end down the centre of the road would have separated traffic travelling in either direction. A raised pavement was located on the southern side of the roadway, which was edged with granite kerbstones.

The goods station platforms and warehousing were concentrated at the western end of the site, extending over Wheler Street. The red brick foundations of the platforms that ran along each railway siding were visible at the time of the survey, as were the dressed stone blocks, with circular recesses in their uppermost surface, which were the foundation stones for the cast iron columns supporting the platform canopies. The hydraulic wagon hoists and their canopies, which had been visible during a visit to the site in 1982 (http://www.subbrit.org.uk/sb-sites/sites/b/bishopsgate_goods_station), had been demolished by the time of the survey.

4.7 The impact of the railway on Shoreditch

In 1886, Charles Booth, philanthropist and social campaigner, began a survey of living and working conditions in London, a project that continued until 1903. The results of the fieldwork undertaken by Booth and his team of researchers were presented in his *Descriptive map of London poverty*, which used a system of colour-coding residential properties to identify the economic and social make-up of each street in London. Booth's study indicates that in 1889 the area through which the railway viaduct passed was mainly occupied by poor and very poor households. More economically and socially mixed households, some financially comfortable and others poor, were concentrated along the main roads, including Brick Lane. Booth's maps of poverty in London were presented as an objective statement, yet can be seen as embodying the subjective attitudes of a middle-class, evangelical social reformer. The information contained in the maps and accompanying reports was gathered by a team of investigators who were recruited largely from Toynbee Hall, a university settlement in Whitechapel. The investigators accompanied School Board Visitors, who had a detailed knowledge of families with children, and policemen on their beats. The notebook of the investigator who accompanied Sergeant French from the Commercial Street police station on 22 March 1898 commented on the dirty appearance of the children in Fleet Street (now the western end of Pedley Street) and that he saw one child who was wearing only one shoe. Thieves and prostitutes who operated in Boundary Street, in the Old Nichol area, congregated at the eastern end of Pedley Street; the Old Nichol was located further west, to the north of Bishopsgate goods station, and was presented as a notorious slum in contemporary newspaper accounts and thinly-disguised fiction such as Arthur Morrison's *A child of the Jago* (1896).

The effect that the insertion of linear features such as roads and railways has on the functioning of a landscape and the people who populate it has been researched by several academics. Urban historian David Reeder pointed out how Charles Booth's *Descriptive map of London poverty* provides information on the impact that spatial forms in London had on the location of economically poor areas. He noted that the map points to the significance especially of innumerable dead ends, closed-up vistas and backwaters in the layout of streets; a more careful reading indicates how some new addition to the ground plan – for example, a dock or canal, a gasworks or waterworks, a railway line, or just the alignment of a new street – seems to have served to reinforce slum tendencies. Booth and his team were repeatedly to draw attention in later volumes to the importance of physical barriers. For example, to the north of Shoreditch 'another dark spot of longstanding poverty and extremely low life … is wedged in between the Regent's Canal and the gas works' (C Booth, cited in Pfautz 1967, 113), and the difficulties involved in navigating through the urban landscape when new barriers such as motorway flyovers are constructed are familiar today (Penrose and Trickett 2004).

The construction of a railway in an urban centre seemed to put a stop to the kind of small-scale development that was crucial to keeping up the standard of housing in its vicinity:

It is conspicuous that where the railways passed no residential improvement took place. They were frozen, as far as renovation or improvement was concerned, as completely as if time had stopped in 1830. Capital sunk in replacing residential housing in such an environment with a more up-to-date equivalent was obviously considered capital wasted. The best plan for a proprietor was to patch the properties up, accept a lower class of tenant, and wait until a major alteration made it possible to abandon residential use altogether: until a commercial or business offer was made, a corporation clearance or street widening scheme swept the district away, or the railways themselves enlarged their approaches. (Kellett 1969, 340)

While the construction of the railway viaduct created a physical barrier, the structure provided a refuge too, in the spaces underneath the arches. There were few restrictions on the activities that could be carried out underneath them (and the few restrictions that were in place were difficult to enforce), and they provided large spaces at little or no financial cost.

The railway arches, particularly those in Grimsby Street, provided shelter for the East End's homeless, and across London railway arches and vaulted spaces afforded shelter for the city's vagrants (Samuel 1973). For many years, the bridges across the Thames served as what were called 'dry arch hotels' for the city's vagrants, and the arches under the Adelphi Buildings, a late 18th-century speculative residential development between the Strand and the Thames, were described as 'a little subterranean city' (Miller 1852, 207), where 'no sane person would have ventured out to explore them without an armed escort' (Shaw 1914, 61–2). Arthur Harding, a reformed petty criminal and contemporary of the Krays, recalled vividly the nights spent sleeping under the Brick Lane bridge as a child:

We got slung out of Drysdale Street because we were three children, and a fourth coming, and there wasn't supposed to be any at all. I remember that quite well. It was rainy, a

January day. The first night we were homeless and settled down under Brick Lane arch for the night. There were others laying there, with sheets of newspaper on the pavement and old coats to cover them. It was a common thing both at Brick Lane arch and Wheler Street, the two railway arches. The Wheler Street arch was more crowded because it was longer and bigger. The police walked down the right-hand side, the people slept on the left. (A Harding, cited in Samuel 1981, 53–4)

For the voyeur, the railway viaduct of the Eastern Counties Railway offered a new way of viewing the inner-city districts of Bethnal Green and Shoreditch, as reported in lurid detail in G W M Reynolds's penny dreadful, *The mysteries of London*:

The traveller upon this line may catch, from the windows of the carriage in which he journeys, a hasty but alas! too comprehensive glance of the wretchedness and squalor of that portion of London. He may actually obtain a view of the interior and domestic misery peculiar to the neighbourhood; he may penetrate with his eyes into the secrets of those abodes of sorrow, vice and destitution. In the summertime the poor always have their windows open, and thus the hideous poverty of their rooms can be readily descried from the summit of the arches on which the railroad is constructed. (Reynolds 1845, cited in Allen 1998, 120)

As Dennis (2008, 334) points out, Reynolds's claims to have observed the women of Shoreditch '… half naked … ironing the linen of a more wealthy neighbour', often 'scolding, swearing and quarrelling', suggests a fertile imagination rather than a 'hasty glance'; but the image is not dissimilar to Gustave Doré's engraving *Over London by rail* (1872), a depiction of what appeared to be the dehumanising effects of 'progress', producing a regimented, industrial-scale townscape (ibid, 335), even though Doré's simplified view masks the complexities of urban living for the poor in the late 19th century (MOL, LIB5788; front cover).

The arches of the Pedley Street and Grimsby Street viaducts played a role in one of London's many trades, the furniture industry. Industry in London has had a complex geography, with some industries concentrated in specific areas and others more widely distributed across the city, with manufacturing being based around small-scale production and finishing trades, undertaken in small workshops or in the home. Historically there was a diverse range of industries in London, but none predominated, unlike metalworking in Birmingham and Sheffield, or textile milling in Lancashire and West Yorkshire. London was a centre for the furniture trade, however, and by the end of the 18th century the City of London and the West End were home to many bespoke manufacturers. During the late 19th century, as the mass market for cheap goods which could be transported across the country emerged, Shoreditch became a focus for the trade in low-priced, ready-made furniture.

While a few large furniture factories were constructed to meet the need for cheap furniture, manufactured on something approaching a production line, the character of the trade required a larger number of small workshops carrying out specialised tasks. This smaller-scale manufacturing could accommodate fluctuations in demand and was more responsive to changing fashions and forms. The various processes involved in production were broken down into stages, each undertaken by a specialised firm. This resulted in a kind of assembly line that ran through the streets of Shoreditch, supplied by a host of ancillary trades that contributed raw materials, machinery, accessories, finishes and warehouses for distribution (Smith and Rogers 2006). There were other advantages to specialised tasks being carried out in the home or in small workshops close to each other; employment in the manufacture of furniture and in other trades was seasonal and on a casual basis, fluctuating with the demands of the market. Rather than being experts in a single trade, some workers would pursue several occupations during the year. Such a pattern of work resulted in workers being spatially dependent, and reliant on local knowledge built up through years of living and working in an area:

The local network played a central part in day-to-day survival when times were difficult, you knew or would quickly hear on the grapevine where to go for cheap or free food and fuel, who would give you credit, where there might be homework given out or a child wanted for errands or child care, what firm was taking on hands, how to get a reference or charitable help. (Davin 1996, 34)

The air raids and population movements of the Second World War brought great disruption to the East End, and the furniture trade went into further significant decline in the 1980s. Firms were unable to keep up with the import of cheaper furniture from overseas, and most of the businesses associated with the Shoreditch furniture trade closed, or relocated to cheaper premises. The few small firms that have remained in the area are run by designers, many of them graduates of the London College of Furniture in Whitechapel, or specialise in high-quality reproduction furniture, such as Barley Reproduction, based in one of the railway arches in Pedley Street until January of 2007 (Fig 75).

The railway arches in Pedley Street and Grimsby Street have had a long history as a place of relative safety and shelter, but their seclusion has also attracted illicit behaviour. Grimsby Street was described by the graffiti artist Banksy as 'a bulletin board for a community', albeit a 'slippery, elusive, anonymous one' (Addley 2006), mainly for reasons of illegality.

In New York and Philadelphia there was a proliferation of graffiti writing on the subways and trains in the late 1970s and early 1980s. The sides of trains made excellent canvases for graffiti, and their mobility meant that graffiti could traverse the city. This 'tagging', a seemingly simple act of spraying one's name, usually takes the form of a stylised signature or logo, which constitutes a language for those who practise it, with its own grammar and syntax (Best 2003, 835). By the mid 1980s, most major European cities, notably Berlin, Paris and

Fig 75 Barley Reproduction, a furniture maker based in one of the railway arches in Pedley Street

Amsterdam, had their own flourishing street art movements, while graffiti emerged from indigenous art forms in South America, particularly Brazil, and later in south-east Asia. Other forms of street art also emerged. In 1981, a French graffiti writer named Blek le Rat began to use the utilitarian method of spraying through stencils, and his spray-painted black rats began to appear on the streets of Paris (Addley 2006).

The anthropologist Nancy Macdonald has studied the syntax and grammar of tagging and found, perhaps not surprisingly, that graffiti attracts graffiti: 'As writers' names hit the wall a form of interaction begins to develop, one which mirrors, on the wall, the activities that might occur in front of it' (Macdonald 2001, 203). Placing one's tag near someone else's is a means of saying 'hello', but writing over the top of another person's tag is a cardinal sin, a violent act. Macdonald suggests that little attention has been paid to the divides that operate within the 'graffiti subculture' – a fractured group that offers its members a diversity of standpoints and realities; its main division centres on how it should present itself to the world. Much of the graffiti in Grimsby Street was more complex than seemingly simple tagging, and involved much larger pieces of contemporary art. During her fieldwork among graffiti writers in London and New York, Macdonald found that professionally undertaken pictorial or abstract work was often discredited for sacrificing the traditional essence of graffiti, as expressed by the graffiti writer Teck:

I made a fair amount of work doing legal art for TV commercials and other film endeavours. In actuality, all of this paled to the thrill of being chased through back streets and narrowingly [sic] escaping the beam of police headlights. Living precariously against the grain took precedence in my daily routine. (*Urb* magazine 37, 1994)

The artworks in Grimsby Street (Fig 76) transcended traditional graffiti methods, and towards the end of the viaduct's life it was used as a canvas by a wider range of artists, beyond the more 'traditional' spray painters. Many of the artistic interventions took the form of stickers, posters and collages, undertaken within the safe (and legal) confines of a studio and then fixed to the walls in Grimsby Street. Some graffiti writers disapprove of such 'nonconformist' activities. Nancy Macdonald's interviews with graffiti writers in New York revealed significant antipathy towards Adam Cost and Revs, two graffiti writers who began producing slogans on stickers and posters which they pasted on walls and street furniture in New York throughout the late 1980s and 1990s. Such measures, which minimise the amount of work required, or which offer a short-cut to fame, are frowned upon, unless the graffiti writer has considerable experience. Despite this, Grimsby Street remained a popular canvas for local and visiting artists. Grimsby Street continued to be appropriated for commercial artistic endeavours; the street and those around it became a popular location for fashion photography shoots and with film-makers, and with so many works by famous (or notorious) contemporary artists covering its walls, Grimsby

Street was a regular stop on organised walking tours of London's graffiti, and a key site to visit in published guides to east London (Bull 2007).

The top of the viaduct, conversely, functioned as a different kind of space. The structure ceased to serve its intended purpose in 1967, following the fire at Bishopsgate goods station and the closure of the Brick Lane goods depot. Appropriation and illicit use of the top of the viaduct was limited to one highly visible structure. Erroneously called a signal box on the various websites devoted to this building, and to other derelict structures in London, the structure was the sludge house for the water-softening plant constructed next to the viaduct in the 1930s (above, 4.3; Fig 53). The Office for Subversive Architecture (OSA) is a loose collective of architects who explore the ways in which people use and interact with public spaces, and address issues relating to urban regeneration by provoking debate and creating awareness of the structures in the built environment. The OSA focuses on areas that tend to be overlooked, forgotten or abandoned; one such project undertaken by the OSA was a refurbishment of the sludge house, which commenced in 2004. The structure reminded the OSA of a stereotypical country cottage, so they decided to restore it as one, painting the exposed concrete exterior of the structure to make it look like a mock Tudor suburban house, wallpapering and furnishing the interior, and installing window boxes filled with artificial geraniums. A light rigged up to a car battery was fitted with a timer, to illuminate the sludge house every evening at 9 o'clock. The transformation was completed in time for London Open House weekend in September 2006, and the popularity of the project

Fig 76 Graffiti in Grimsby Street

was such that a short film was made for broadcast on Channel 4 (*The subversive architects*, 2006).

4.8 The Bishopsgate stampede, and racial tension in Brick Lane

On the night of 28 January 1918 an aerial bombing raid took place over London. Air raids were a regular occurrence during the First World War, with bombs dropped by Zeppelins and then, from 1917 onwards, by Gotha bomber planes (Fig 77). While the bombing was not carried out with the same intensity as that experienced by London and other British towns and cities during the Second World War, the limited number of British planes for defence, combined with the novelty of this type of warfare and the relative quietness of the bomber

aircraft, meant that raids often got through to London with very little warning, causing uncertainty and panic. This was a new and frightening experience for Londoners, as homes, businesses and lives were destroyed by a new kind of warfare.

As the war progressed, methods of warning the populace of approaching Zeppelins and Gothas were developed. Sirens and policemen's whistles and rattles could not be heard above the general din of traffic (Anon 1918), and so by 1918 motor cars cruised the streets firing rockets, or 'maroons', which emitted a loud bang and a bright flash; such devices were, however, themselves often mistaken for exploding bombs (Charlton 1936, 95). Due to the relatively small number of air raids, at least at the beginning of the war, the government decided not to commission purpose-built air-raid shelters, instead encouraging the use of basements, large buildings and underground stations as public shelters by those who found themselves out in the street at the time of a raid (Fig 78). It was at one such shelter, at Bishopsgate goods station, that 14 people were killed on the

Fig 77 *A Gotha bomber plane, 1920 (2665050, Hulton Archive/Getty Images)*

Fig 78 The Underworld *by the official war artist Walter Bayes (1869–1956), depicting Elephant and Castle underground station in use as an air-raid shelter during the First World War (IWM, ART 935, by permission of the Imperial War Museum)*

aforementioned night of 28 January 1918.

The minutes of a meeting of the War Cabinet the next morning (TNA: PRO, CAB/23/5) stated that a total of between 40 and 50 people had been killed in the air raid, during which Gotha bomber planes progressed across the city from east to west (this figure was later revised to 58 deaths, with 173 injured). Thirty deaths were caused when a bomb fell directly on top of an air-raid shelter in Long Acre, near Covent Garden, but the deaths at Bishopsgate goods station were caused when the firing of a 'maroon' rocket was mistaken for an exploding bomb, and panic ensued. People in the streets and buildings in the immediate area rushed for the shelter, including those waiting in the queue for the evening performance at the Olympia music hall on the opposite side of Shoreditch High Street (Hook 1995, 8). A later account, published in London's *Evening News* in March 1935, reported that the two iron gates at the entrance to the goods station were locked, and people were forced against them by the press of the crowd behind. A railway policeman opened one gate, and the crowd surged through the opening, knocking some to the ground. A Mrs Silverstone, who had been a girl at the time of the stampede, gave her account of the events:

We lived near Bishopsgate Goods Station in January 1918 and when we got the warning through on the 28th, the night of the Bishopsgate panic, my elder sister ran off with the baby to the Station. I dressed my brother, who had a bad leg and couldn't walk. I had to carry him on my back, with Mum hanging on behind. Dad would *not* leave the house. He was an old soldier ... The screams of the many hundreds trying to crowd through the gates of the goods station to seek shelter under the railway arches were heart-rending. Maroons were going off and I could see there was no earthly chance of getting in, so we two ran back home. We had only just got in when we heard the crash of a bomb. Dad suggested playing the piano to drown the noise, so I did ... We were worried about my sister and the baby; we found them later amongst the casualties. They were not badly hurt but the next-door neighbour lost his wife, two children and his mother-in-law. (Mrs R Silverstone, in a letter to the *Evening News*, 5 March 1935, cited in Hook 1995, 8)

Two men, six women and six children were trampled to death (Table 8) and a further 14 were injured.

As the First World War had progressed, the War Cabinet recognised the drain on morale that German bombing caused, and it was decided to restrict the wholesale reporting of air raids. *The Times* newspaper of 29 January 1918, the morning after the raid, did not report the stampede, or any other deaths or damage caused by bombing, but did emphasise the good-natured and stoic manner in which Londoners had dealt with adversity the previous night, and British military success in bringing down an enemy aeroplane. Nevertheless, the impact of the air raids on an increasingly war-weary population resulted in a major drop in the productivity of London industry; in explaining the 87.5% reduction in output in the East End's

factories, Mr H M Selby, the managing director of Schneider and Sons, 'the largest clothing manufacturers in England', pointed out that '90% of the employees were women, easily frightened and liable to panic' and that 'the other 10% were alien Jews, who were even more liable to panic than the women' (cited in Harvey 1992, 397–8). Government officials and the press happily accepted and propagated statements that Jewish immigrants were more demoralised by the air raids than non-Jews.

At their meeting at 10 Downing Street the morning after the stampede at Bishopsgate goods station, members of the War Cabinet expressed the opinion that if the panic at the station were to be mentioned in a press report, 'attention should be drawn to the fact that the stampede occurred among foreign-born inhabitants' (TNA: PRO, CAB/23/5, 2). These 'foreign-born inhabitants' were London's Russian Jews and their descendants, large numbers of whom had fled eastern Europe after the assassination of Tsar Alexander II in March 1881 sparked off pogroms, or riots and attacks, against the Jewish population, who had been blamed in the press for the assassination. Further anti-Semitic pogroms occurred between 1903 and 1906 in the Russian Pale of Settlement, the western part of Imperial Russia where Jews were permitted to reside, during which thousands of Jews were killed. One of the worst atrocities occurred in 1905 in the town of Odessa, in present-day Ukraine, where there were reports of the deaths of up to 2500 Jews. These events caused the large-scale migration of Jews westwards, many ultimately aiming for North America, although significant numbers only ever made it as far as London (Rischin 1987, 29).

With the resulting increase in population in east London during the late 19th and early 20th centuries, and the impact that this was perceived as having on the availability of jobs and homes, attitudes towards the Jews of the East End turned from ambivalence to overt antipathy (Kershen 2005, 191). Distinctions were made between the settled Anglo-Jewish community, who had resided in London since Oliver Cromwell

Table 8 Deaths caused during the stampede at Bishopsgate goods station, 28 January 1918

Name	Age
Louis Beltisky	5
Woolf Bider	70
Hettie Bodie	18 months
Cassie Bodie	5
Fanny Bodie	28
Millie Cohen	58
Marx Green	7
Rosa Green	14
Kate Greenland	47
Abraham Hankin	6 months
Esther Harris	60
Rachel Sax	48
Isidore Schagrin	75
Rachel Shultosky	30

readmitted Jews to England in 1656, and those who were 'foreign' or, more particularly, 'alien', the frequently used pejorative term for eastern European Jewish immigrants. The word 'alien' conveyed to late 19th- and early 20th-century newspaper readers and others the distinct nature of pauper immigrants who seemed foreign, and out of harmony with the characteristics and behaviour of the English (ibid, 192).

Accounts of the inquests into the 14 deaths in the stampede at Bishopsgate goods station duly appeared, including one in the *East London Advertiser* headlined 'Cowardly Aliens in the Great Stampede' (Harvey 1992, 398), and another in *The Times* reporting the coroner's statement that:

[T]he deaths appeared to have been due to panic almost entirely on the part of persons who might be called foreigners, or who were of foreign extraction. One could have hoped that people living in London would by this time have regained their powers of self-confidence and control – qualities which would have enabled them to act very differently and not in a way unworthy of men and more nearly approaching the ways of the lower animals. (Anon 1918)

Londoners reading such reports could be in no doubt that those referred to were members of the Jewish community.

The cultural stereotyping was taken even further. The newspaper reports of the inquests carefully itemised the quantities of money, gold, investment certificates and jewellery that the dead were carrying, and, in the same report in *The Times* as quoted above, the coroner and police witness drew attention to the fact that the crowd contained a 'vast number of men of military age, nearly all of whom were of Russian nationality'. Many Russian Jewish men received certificates of exemption from war service from the Russian Embassy, but many others joined the British Army (White 2003, 244) or returned to Russia to fight there; the father of the writer and poet Emanuel Litvinoff, who grew up in Fuller Street in Bethnal Green, to the north of the Great Eastern Railway line, returned to Russia to join the army; Emanuel and his family never heard from him again (Litvinoff 1972).

Racial tensions continued to be expressed in the Brick Lane area throughout the 20th century, and the railway bridge over Brick Lane provided a focal point (Fig 79). Street corners and open spaces in the street were assembly points for Jewish socialists and anarchists, and the mid 1930s saw battles with Oswald Mosley's British Union of Fascists. The railway bridge marked the boundary between the predominantly Jewish (and later Bengali) stretch of Brick Lane to the south, and the 'white English' environment of Bethnal Green to the north; in recalling the Brick Lane of their youth in the 1920s and 1930s, Sara and Maurice 'Pip' Goldstein 'generally … didn't go past the railway bridge' (Sara Goldstein, cited in Lichtenstein 2007, 244), as doing so would have risked racial abuse, or worse, from the gangs of fascist youths who patrolled the area (ibid, 23).

Fig 79 The railway bridge over Brick Lane, c 1976, looking south (© J Connor/Tower Hamlets Local History Library and Archives, LH82/70/30)

The role of Brick Lane bridge as a boundary and flashpoint between communities lasted beyond the Depression era of the 1930s: '[in the 1970s] you hardly ever saw Bengalis north of the bridge. It was almost as if there were two Brick Lanes' (Rev Kenneth Leech, cited in Lichtenstein 2007, 45), and until the mid 1990s the Brick Lane railway bridge was a favoured haunt for representatives of the National Front, who would 'swear and spit at any Bengalis that walked past' (Kershen 2005, 213). The Bangladesh Liberation War of 1971 led to large numbers of people from the Sylhet region fleeing to Britain, and an exile community grew in the Brick Lane area; by the late 1970s the Bangladeshi community had largely replaced the declining Jewish community that had begun to settle there 90 years before. A reprise of the racial tensions of the 1930s occurred, with growing numbers of racially motivated attacks on Bangladeshis. In May 1978, the murder of the 25-year-old Bangladeshi garment worker Altab Ali by three teenage boys at the corner of Adler Street and Whitechapel Road, close to the southern end of Brick Lane, mobilised the community (Keith 2005, 144). Demonstrations were held in Brick Lane and the surrounding area against the National Front and racial violence (Fig 80).

From the 1990s a new, artistic, community made Brick Lane its home. 'Banglatown', a concentration of restaurants, food shops and clothing wholesalers, was still located towards the southern end of the street in Whitechapel, but the former Truman Brewery in the centre of the street had been converted into offices, bars and studios, and many of the new generation of 'Young British Artists' established studios in the vicinity, including Tracey Emin and Sarah Lucas's 'The Shop' at 103 Bethnal Green Road.

As we neared the Bethnal Green end of the street I was aware that something felt different, the street had opened up somehow, it was changed. Then I realised why: the railway bridge had gone. The site of so many encounters over the centuries, the place of conflict and passion, the almost physical divide between communities, had disappeared … A negative impression of the bridge hung across the street. I felt myself instinctively hunch as we walked through the former dark shadows underneath. (Lichtenstein 2007, 255)

Fig 80 Gathering for a demonstration in Brick Lane, organised by the Bengali Youth Movement Against Racism, June 1978 (London Metropolitan University East End Archive: The Paul Trevor Collection, B-317-09 © Paul Trevor 2011)

5

The origins and development of the East London line

The East London line largely owes its existence to the design and construction of the Thames Tunnel and to its subsequent failure as a commercial enterprise. The Thames Tunnel is the oldest part of the infrastructure of the London Underground, and was designed and constructed at great expense by the French-born engineer Marc Brunel, assisted by his son Isambard Kingdom Brunel, between 1825 and 1843.

When the tunnel was constructed it was intended to provide a much-needed vehicle and pedestrian crossing between the northern and southern banks of the Thames. Until Westminster Bridge was completed in 1750, London Bridge was the only bridge crossing the Thames in London; the Corporation of London and the Bridge House Estates protected their rights over the tolls charged to cross the bridge, preventing the construction of other crossings until the middle of the 18th century. Until the construction of multiple river crossings it was quicker for most people crossing the river to use ferries or river taxis (wherries), which could be hailed by standing on the bank or at the river stairs dotted along both sides of the Thames (Roberts 2005, 4–5).

During the late 18th and early 19th centuries, several new bridges were opened, at Blackfriars (1769), Vauxhall (1816), Waterloo (1817) and Southwark (1819). London Bridge remained the most easterly point at which vehicles could cross the Thames, however, and it was in poor repair and struggled to cope with the traffic using the crossing. On one day in July 1811, a traffic census recorded 89,640 pedestrians, 2924 carts and drays, 1240 coaches, 769 wagons, and 764 horses and gigs and taxed carts passing over London Bridge; the eastwards expansion of London, and the development of the docks at Wapping, Rotherhithe and the East India Dock on the Isle of Dogs, had put a tremendous strain on London Bridge (Watson 2004, 52). The bridge was damaged by the severe winter of 1813–14, when the river froze over for a long period of time and the last frost fair was held. Construction of a new bridge, designed and built by John Rennie, commenced in 1824 and was completed in 1831.

Long before the rebuilding of London Bridge, there had been a number of attempts at constructing a tunnel beneath the Thames; a tunnel was preferred over a new bridge, as a bridge span would have to have been of sufficient height to allow tall-masted ships to pass under it, to reach the Pool of London beyond, and steam engine technology had not progressed sufficiently to allow a bridge deck to be raised and lowered, like that later used for Tower Bridge. At the end of the 18th century, the engineer Ralph Dodd proposed a road tunnel underneath the Thames estuary between Tilbury Fort in Essex and Gravesend in Kent. An Act of Parliament enabling work to commence was passed in July 1799, and work on the tunnel began in May 1801. Work had to be abandoned two years later, however, leaving only a shaft 80ft deep, dug at a cost of £15,000, to show for Dodd's efforts (Lee 1976, 7).

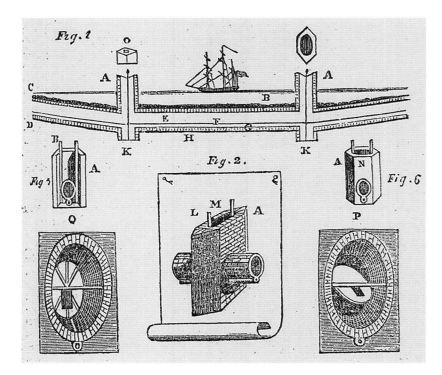

Fig 81 *Mr Hawkins's plan for a tunnel under the Thames* (Mechanic's Mag, *6 December 1823, University of Bristol Library*)

By 1823 Marc Brunel had devised a tunnelling shield which would be capable of tunnelling through the soft, unreliable ground below the Thames, and he published his ideas in the *Mechanic's Magazine* in September 1823, raising awareness of and financial support for his project. Various other designs for a tunnel were published by both amateur and professional engineers (Anon 1823; Johnson 1823; Fig 81; Fig 82), but it was Marc Brunel's design which received the Royal Assent in June 1824 (Matthewson et al 2006, 29).

Construction of the tunnel began with the sinking of a vertical brick shaft at Rotherhithe; the shaft was constructed above ground as a tower, mounted on top of a cast-iron 'curb', which acted as a blade, cutting through the ground. The shaft would, in theory, sink into the ground under its own weight, and the spoil from the interior of the shaft would be taken away by means of a bucket chain powered by a steam engine. Arrangements were made with a local landowner for the spoil to be carried away from the tunnel excavations on a railway and dumped on his land, and for a brickworks to be constructed there.

Once the shaft had eventually been sunk to the required depth, foundations were constructed below the shaft, along with an opening for the tunnelling shield. The tunnelling shield consisted of a frame containing three rows of 12 cells, each of which was manned by a labourer who removed the spoil from in front of him using a pickaxe. The spoil was carried along the tunnel to Rotherhithe, and once a sufficient amount of earth had been removed, the tunnelling shield would be inched forward. The newly-excavated tunnel was then lined with brick

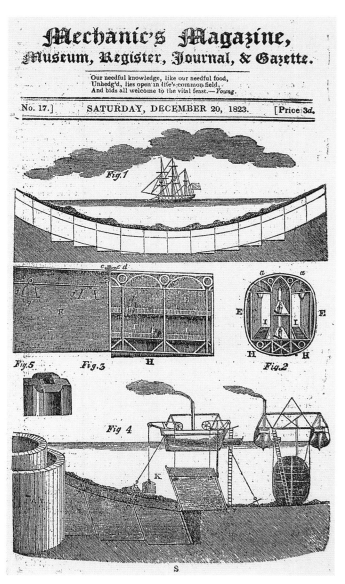

Fig 82 *Mr Johnson's alternative plan for an iron tunnel under the Thames* (Mechanic's Mag, *20 December 1823, University of Bristol Library*)

and 'Roman' cement.

As tunnelling progressed further under the River Thames, increasing amounts of water entered the tunnel, and there were several serious inundations. In January 1828, water rushed in through the tunnelling shield, killing six men and injuring many others, including Isambard Kingdom Brunel who was assisting his father Marc with the design and construction of the tunnel. Within 15 minutes all 600ft (183m) of the tunnel had been flooded (Fig 83).

Construction of the tunnel ceased in August 1828, and the entrance to the tunnel was bricked up. The search for further funds began, and construction recommenced in 1835. The Thames Tunnel eventually opened to great fanfare in 1843, and was described at the time as the eighth wonder of the world. Visitors flocked to the tunnel, where they could buy souvenirs from stalls set up along its length, and each year a 'Fancy Fair' featuring scientific demonstrations, musical performers and sideshows was held in the tunnel (Fig 84).

Such was the excitement surrounding the construction of the tunnel that, from the earliest days of the venture, souvenir etchings were produced of the completed tunnel, showing the spiral ramps that would be used by the horses pulling carts and carriages. The tunnel was even shown in its completed state on contemporary maps, such as the Greenwoods' map surveyed between 1824 and 1826 (Fig 85) when the tunnel was still in the earliest stages of construction (Greenwood and Greenwood 1827).

By the 1860s, however, the tunnel had become a dangerous place of ill-repute. Funds had run out before the spiral ramps for horses and carriages could be constructed, so the tunnel could only be used for pedestrian traffic, reducing the anticipated revenue. Despite being an engineering success, the tunnel was an economic failure and never recouped the investments made in it; in 1865 the tunnel was purchased by the East London Railway Company for £200,000 (Wolmar 2005, 101).

Fig 83 The inundation of the Thames Tunnel on 12 January 1828 (Brunel Museum, Rotherhithe, LDBRU2002.2)

Fig 84 An advertisement for entertainments at the Thames Tunnel, 1857 (private collection; reproduction rights held by the Brunel Museum, Rotherhithe)

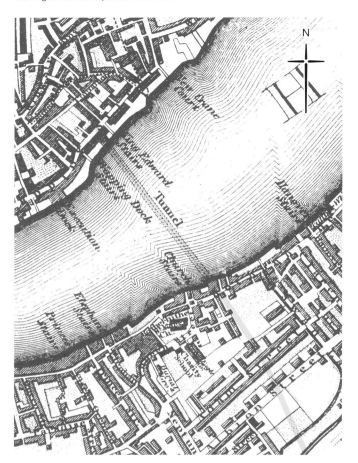

Fig 86 Wapping, Rotherhithe and the East London Railway on the 1st edition Ordnance Survey map of 1878 (scale 1:2500)

Fig 85 The Greenwoods' map of London, surveyed between 1824 and 1826, showing the Thames Tunnel as it would have appeared when completed (Greenwood and Greenwood 1827) (scale 1:7920)

5.2   The opening of the East London Railway

The chairman of the East London Railway, which later became the East London line of the London Underground, proposed that the Thames Tunnel should be used as part of a new railway line between Shoreditch station and the London and Brighton Railway line at New Cross in south-east London; this railway would connect the Wapping Docks on the northern side of the River Thames with the Surrey Commercial Docks and railway marshalling yards of New Cross on the southern side of the river. The East London Railway Company was a consortium of six railway companies comprising the Great Eastern Railway (GER), the London, Brighton and South Coast Railway (LB&SCR), the London, Chatham and Dover Railway (LCDR), the South Eastern Railway (SER), the Metropolitan Railway and the Metropolitan District Railway. The last two companies operated what are now the Metropolitan, District, Circle, and Hammersmith and City lines of the London Underground.

The railway line between Wapping and New Cross (now New Cross Gate) was constructed by way of a cut-and-cover tunnel, with the line being uncovered to the south of the Surrey Docks, and opened in 1869. At the time of construction,

the northern bank of the Thames was intensively developed with warehouses, workshops, factories and housing, but the southern bank had not yet been built up in such an intensive way (Fig 86). The streets immediately adjacent to the Thames waterfront were crammed with warehouses and housing, but land to the south, near the Surrey Commercial Docks, was still largely undeveloped, facilitating the construction of a cut-and-cover tunnel.

In 1876 the railway was extended further north to Shoreditch station, near Brick Lane, with intermediate stations at Whitechapel and Shadwell. A rail link to the Great Eastern Railway Company's lines into Liverpool Street station was also constructed. Much of the railway extension was, like the rest of the line, constructed in a cut-and-cover tunnel, running below existing streets, although some rows of terraced housing in Shadwell and Whitechapel were demolished and their occupants displaced. During the early years of the railways, 'through-running', where trains could use the tracks and stations of other companies to provide a greater range of services, was more common, and it was possible to take a train from Liverpool Street to Brighton, or from New Cross to Kensington, using the ELR (Lee 1976, 26). Among the posters and leaflets produced by the railway companies in Yiddish for the East End's Jewish community were handbills containing information about travelling to the Crystal Palace on the ELR (Fig 87), and other opportunities for day-trips to the south coast. The importance of Jewish passengers to railway companies across the country during the late 19th and early

Fig 87 A handbill in Yiddish advertising the East London Railway's reduced-price ticket, combining return travel from Shoreditch, Whitechapel and Shadwell with entrance to the Crystal Palace for 1s 6d, c 1901 (LTM, 1998/43369, © TfL from the London Transport Museum collection)

20th centuries, a time when there was a mass movement of Jews from the Russian Pale of Settlement across Europe, many heading towards North America in order to escape the pogroms (Chapter 4.8), is demonstrated by the large numbers of posters and handbills written in Yiddish that the companies supplied.

The total cost of the construction of the railway in 1876 was £3.2 million, and extension of the line north of Wapping had involved an extensive programme of engineering works. The ELR was to be carried below the London Dock Basin, to the north of Wapping, necessitating the construction of a tunnel. The London Dock Company stipulated that the dock would have to be maintained for use by shipping throughout the construction process, so a cofferdam, spanning half of the dock, was constructed. The area of the dock contained within the dam was drained and the twin tunnels of the ELR constructed. The dam was then removed, a second cofferdam built, the second half of the dock drained, and the remainder of the tunnel under the dock constructed. The railway tunnel

continued under a sugar warehouse which was located on the northern side of the London Dock, and this was described by Sir John Hawkshaw, the railway company engineer as

… a work requiring great care, as the warehouse had basements and the floors over the basements were entirely supported on groined brick arches. The brick piers supporting these arches were all underpinned with concrete as far down as the foundation of the tunnel itself, after which the ground was excavated between the piers, and the basement then presented a most striking appearance when illuminated by the lights of the warehouse, the groined brick arches being supported on columns 60 feet high. The brickwork of the tunnel was built around and among these concrete columns, which were afterwards removed wholly from within the tunnel, and the concrete, where it passed through the brickwork, was then cut out and replaced by brickwork. (cited in Lee 1976, 14)

Construction of the tunnel below the docks was not completed on time, and compensation of £45,000 was paid to the London Dock Company. The construction of the railway below the existing viaduct of the London and Blackwall Railway in Shadwell required the underpinning of seven of the viaduct piers to a depth of 60ft. In 1880 a spur of the railway was constructed to what is now New Cross station, and intermediate stations at Deptford Road (now Surrey Quays) and Rotherhithe opened in 1884.

Charles Booth's *Descriptive map of London poverty* of 1889 (Chapter 4.7) conveys the Victorian perception of the economic and social character of the areas through which the ELR passed. The cut-and-cover tunnel constructed north of Wapping did not present the kind of physical barrier that Booth had blamed for creating pockets of poverty, cutting off streets and communities from the main thoroughfares where the homes of the professional classes were concentrated (coloured in red on his maps), but the railway did pass through an area of historically great poverty, as signified by the buildings coloured in dark blue ('Very poor, casual. Chronic want') and black ('Lowest class. Vicious, semi-criminal'). It was these same areas, close to the industry of the East End and the docks on both sides of the River Thames, which were badly bombed during the Second World War.

In 1913 the ELR was electrified (Fig 88), rendering the cylindrical brick air vents dotted along the route redundant, although most of them still remain today. In 1933 the ELR, along with other underground railways, came under the control of the London Passenger Transport Board, the organisation with responsibility for public transport within London. The railway became the 'East London Branch' of the Metropolitan line. The East London line's situation, on what was the eastern edge of the London Underground network, meant that it was often left off the early underground railways maps. The lines and stations on early underground maps were laid out geographically, and often superimposed on top of road maps, meaning that central London stations were shown close together and those in the suburbs as far apart. Lack of space meant that nothing other

Fig 88 A poster produced by the Underground Electric Railway Company in 1913, advertising the newly electrified line (LTM, 1983/4/361, © TfL from the London Transport Museum collection)

Fig 89 A poster produced by London Underground in 1990 to advertise the East London line's change in colour and new separate identity (LTM, 1990/76, © TfL from the London Transport Museum collection)

than the central London stations were shown on pocket maps.

The iconic Tube map designed by Harry Beck, an engineering draughtsman at the London Underground Signals Office, showed the East London line in the same colour as the Metropolitan line until 1990, when it was first depicted in the colour orange, giving the East London line its own separate identity (Fig 89). The flexibility of Harry Beck's design meant that changes could be made to colours, connections and stations, and whole lines added or removed, without damaging the overall legibility of the map.

5.3   The East London line and its stations

Shoreditch underground station

Shoreditch underground station (Fig 90) opened on 10 April 1876, and was linked via a short stretch of track to Liverpool Street station. A difficult relationship with the Great Eastern

Railway meant that the link saw little use, and once the East London Railway was electrified in 1913, the link could no longer be used; the station's southbound platform was rendered redundant, and was demolished in *c* 1963, although not before it was turned into flowerbeds by the staff of the London Underground, who took great pride in keeping the station presentable (Fig 91). Services from the station were reduced from the 1950s, however, as the riverside docks the line served went into decline. Saturday services were finally withdrawn in October 1966 (London Transport Museum 2002); the observant Jews of Shoreditch and Spitalfields would not have used the station during the *Shabbat*, which lasts from sunset on Friday until Saturday evening, and for this reason markets in the area, including those in Brick Lane, Columbia Road and Middlesex Street (formerly Petticoat Lane), were held on Sundays (Fig 92).

Shoreditch underground station was constructed of yellow stock brick, which at the time of the survey had been recently sand-blasted and repointed. The main station building, containing the ticket hall and offices, was single-

Fig 90 The exterior of Shoreditch underground station in Pedley Street, looking west

Fig 91 Mrs Metherall, the station porter at Shoreditch, was awarded 3rd prize in the Metropolitan line section of the station gardens competition in 1945 (LTM, 1998/48134, © TfL from the London Transport Museum collection)

storeyed with a single pitched slate roof and arched window openings, a 19th-century gaslight bracket mounted over the station entrance, and cast iron guttering. A modern London Underground roundel sign was located over the main entrance doors, which had a fanlight (covered over with vertical timber boarding) and a stone threshold step. The station building extended over the tracks of the East London line, being carried on riveted wrought iron plate girders which were supported by the brick cutting walls (Fig 93).

The interior of the booking hall had undergone some alteration since it was photographed in the 1950s (Fig 94). The glazed timber screen of the ticket office had been removed and a stainless steel screen installed in its place (Fig 95), and the panelled timber doors replaced with fire doors. Double-leaf doors led to the staircase lobby and bridge spanning the tracks.

Whitechapel station

Whitechapel station (Fig 96) opened in 1876, with deep-level platforms serving the ELR. The Metropolitan District Railway (now the District line of the London Underground) opened a new station adjacent to the ELR in 1884, which at the time acted as the terminus for an extension of the railway line from

Fig 92 The Sunday market in Brick Lane, 1976 (London Metropolitan University East End Archive: The Paul Trevor Collection, B-120-17, © Paul Trevor 2011)

Fig 93 The platforms and ticket hall of Shoreditch underground station, looking west

Fig 94 The booking hall of Shoreditch underground station in June 1955 (LTM, 1998/65115, © TfL from the London Transport Museum collection)

Fig 95 The booking hall of Shoreditch underground station in 2006

Mansion House. The brick cutting walls contained arched refuge recesses for personnel working on the line; the recesses were subsequently rendered unusable when cables for electrical supply and communication were fixed to the cutting walls, crossing the recesses.

Shadwell station

The present Shadwell station is located in Cable Street and was built in 1983 to replace the first station, which opened as part of the northwards extension of the ELR in 1876. The first ticket hall building (Fig 97) was very similar to that at Shoreditch, and was located in Watney Street, with an emergency exit in the northern side of the London and Blackwall Railway's viaduct in Chapman Street. The station was renamed 'Shadwell and St George-in-the-East' in 1900, but reverted to its original name in 1918. The platforms at Shadwell were in part illuminated by a lightwell and ventilation shaft to the south of the station, which was spanned by cast iron bracing beams supporting the brick walls of the cutting, where there was no brick vault.

In 1983, a new ticket hall with lifts for disabled access was constructed in Cable Street, over what had formerly been an open shaft. The redundant ticket hall in Watney Street and its associated disused staircases, which were reached from doors that opened straight out on to the centre of each platform, were left in place. The stairs were constructed of concrete and had cylindrical steel handrails; one staircase had led to the emergency exit in Chapman Street (above).

Wapping station

Wapping station was constructed around the brick entrance shaft of the Thames Tunnel on the northern bank of the Thames. The station originally opened as the northern terminus of the ELR in 1869, and a booking hall was constructed in Wapping High Street (Fig 98). Much of the original structure of the tunnel entrance shaft was retained and converted for use in the new station. The polygonal structure with its decorative pilasters visible above ground was retained, and the station platforms were accessed via the spiral staircases originally installed for the pedestrians using the Thames Tunnel. At the base of the entrance shaft, opposite the entrance to the Thames Tunnel, the brick lining of the shaft was broken through and a short length of tunnel was excavated to form the station platforms; an open shaft extending across the tracks was constructed to allow the steam and smoke produced by the trains to escape. Brick retaining walls with counterforts were constructed to either side of the cutting. Ordinarily, a retaining wall would have required buttresses to prevent the weight of the earth behind the wall from pushing it over, but these would have impinged on the running of the railway, so counterforts were developed. The vertical brick retaining walls of the open shaft incorporated

Fig 96 The platforms of Whitechapel station

arched recesses, into which were set curving walls which sloped downwards towards the base of the wall. To provide additional stability, cast iron struts were fitted to the retaining walls, spanning the tracks (Fig 99).

A passenger lift, which ran down the centre of the Wapping shaft, was installed in 1915. Like many buildings which stood adjacent to the docks of east London, Wapping station was badly damaged by bombing during the Second

Fig 97 The exterior of Shadwell station, looking north-west

Fig 98 The exterior of Wapping station in 1934 (LTM, 1998/56043, © TfL from the London Transport Museum collection)

World War, when incendiaries hit the surrounding warehouses (Fig 100). Only the polygonal entrance shaft was left above ground, and debris had fallen down the shaft and on to the tracks. For several years a timber shed served as the ticket hall for the station, before it was rebuilt in the 1950s.

Rotherhithe station

Rotherhithe station (Fig 101) opened in 1884, close to the southern end of the Thames Tunnel, although unlike Wapping station, Rotherhithe did not incorporate the tunnel's southern stair shaft as part of the station. The station frontage was rebuilt and extended forwards in 1905–6, the former front elevation being replaced with two decorated cast iron columns.

Surrey Quays station

Surrey Quays station (Fig 102) opened in 1884, when it was named 'Deptford Road'; the station changed its name to 'Surrey Docks' in 1911 and received its present name in 1989, when the Surrey Quays shopping centre opened at the site of the former Surrey Docks. The station was not contained within a cut-and-cover tunnel, unlike Rotherhithe, Wapping and Shadwell, but instead the platforms were open to the air and contained within a brick cutting. The cutting walls of Surrey Quays station incorporated arched recessed refuges for railway personnel working on the line; these had been rendered useless when communication and electrical cables were fixed to the cutting walls.

Fig 99 The counterfort retaining walls and cast iron struts at Wapping station

Fig 100 The exterior of Wapping station in October 1940 after sustaining damage during an air raid, looking south-east (LTM, 1998/48904, © TfL from the London Transport Museum collection)

Fig 101 The platforms of Rotherhithe station

Fig 102 The platforms of Surrey Quays station

The Cope Street and Rotherhithe New Road bridges

Cope Street had been constructed by 1862, when Stanford's map of that year shows it under its original name of Cross Street, between Rotherhithe Lower Road and Baltic Place. The 1st edition Ordnance Survey map of 1868 shows that it incorporated what appears to be the present bridge over the

ELR line to New Cross station (now New Cross Gate). In 1875 the street changed to its present name of Cope Street. The bridge deck (Fig 103; Fig 104) was constructed of cast iron beams with intermediate brick jack-arches carried on brick piers on the eastern and western sides of the railway cutting, and a central bracing frame which comprised open-ended cast iron boxes bolted to each other.

Fig 103 The Cope Street bridge, looking north

Fig 104 Detail of the cast iron structure and brick jack-arches of the Cope Street bridge

Rotherhithe New Road had been constructed as a short-cut across the loop in Corbets Lane and Plough Lane by 1862. A bridge had been constructed to carry the road over the ELR line by 1868 and, as with the Cope Street bridge, the road deck was formed by cast iron beams with intermediate brick jack-arches supported on brick piers on the eastern and western sides of the cutting, and a central cast iron bracing frame.

5.4 Conclusion

The East London Railway, which subsequently became the East London line of the London Underground, was part of a second wave of railway construction in the capital, which from the 1850s and 1860s aimed to link up London's disparate communities and industries. The railway mainlines of the 1830s and 1840s sought to straddle the country, and transport people and goods over long distances, rather than linking the city with what were then outlying villages, and the first intermediate stations on the early mainlines were some distance from London. Despite the railways' impact on the country, and on perceptions of distance and time, 'until the 1860s … their least important impact was in providing transport within London itself' (Weightman and Humphries 1983, 99).

The ELR, like other underground railways, was significantly different from the suburban railways being constructed at the time, in that the streets had to be closed, a section at a time, while the cut-and-cover tunnels of the railway were being constructed, and adjacent houses, factories, warehouses, viaducts, and even docks, shored up. The railway was built through what was, on the north bank of the River Thames at least, a heavily congested area, packed with rows of terraced housing and industry. Buried out of sight, London's underground railways appear to have remained out of mind during the 19th century (Simmons 1995, 23–5); with the exception of civil engineers and architects, who excitedly discussed aspects of the construction of the subterranean railway network in specialist journals, very few full contemporary accounts of the capital's underground railways were published, an exception being a German publication, *Die Londoner Untergrundbahnen* by Ludwig Troske, which appeared in 1892. While the early railway mainlines of the 1830s and 1840s had inspired awe-struck accounts by travel writers, the workaday urban and suburban railways of 20 years later were taken more for granted by Londoners.

6

Dalston and the North London Railway

'[A] crowded down-at-heel thoroughfare with plenty of character, if not much architecture'
Cherry and Pevsner 1998, 508

6.1 Dalston: a village outside the city

In the mid 18th century Dalston was a small hamlet midway along Dalston Lane, approximately 2 miles (3.2km) from the edge of the City of London. The village stood close to another settlement, Kingsland, a group of houses arranged along what is now Kingsland Road and Kingsland High Street, along the route of Ermine Street, the Roman road from London to York. The Stamford Hill turnpike trust was established in 1713 in order to run a toll road between Shoreditch and Enfield along this stretch of Ermine Street, and a toll gate was constructed at Kingsland Green, now the junction of Kingsland Road, Dalston Lane, Kingsland High Street and Balls Pond Road. During the 18th century Kingsland was the larger of the two settlements, boosted by its position on the main road from London to the north; in 1733 there were five inns in Kingsland and only two in Dalston. The village of Kingsland was subsumed by Dalston, and the name came to denote the built-up area on the eastern side of Kingsland High Street (*VCH* 1995, 28). Despite the comparative ease with which one could reach the city from Kingsland and Dalston in the 18th century, the land to either side of Kingsland Road was largely devoid of housing, and instead was developed as market gardens and for use as brickfields; the bricks used to build the houses between Shoreditch and Dalston, and the viaduct of the North London Railway, most likely came from these fields.

In the late 18th and early 19th centuries Dalston was well known for its nurseries, which extended southwards from Dalston Lane. Maps from the early 19th century such as the Greenwoods' map of London (Greenwood and Greenwood 1827) and Starling's map of Hackney of 1831 (Fig 105) show that Dalston was being gradually developed as an attractive place for the middling sort to live, being within comparatively easy reach of the city. A number of large brick terraces of houses, including Dalston Terrace, Kingsland Place and Warwick Place, had been constructed along Kingsland Road. The Regent's Canal, to the south of Dalston, had been completed in 1820 and, along with the docks and warehouses that grew up along its length, provided an effective barrier against the northwards expansion of the industrial city.

A local family, the Tyssens, had quarried brickearth from an area to the north of the junction of Dalston Lane and Kingsland High Street for building by 1814, and terraced houses had been constructed by the early 19th century along Kingsland Road and Dalston Lane, while to the west of Kingsland Road the De Beauvoir Estate was being constructed. In Samuel Lewis's *A topographical dictionary of England* of 1849, Dalston was described as a 'recently increased suburban village, with some handsome old houses' (Lewis 1849, 4).

Nos 5–13 Roseberry Place

Nos 5–13 Roseberry Place (Fig 106; Fig 107) formed a terrace of five two-storey cottages constructed in the 1840s, predating the arrival of the North London Railway. Each house originally had an entrance hall with a staircase to the first floor, and doors led from the hall to two rooms on the ground floor, one with a window at the front of the house and one at the rear. The terrace was constructed of brick with rendered border detailing around the external door and window openings; the east-facing external facade of 7 Roseberry Place had been rendered with cement, and the exterior of each house had been painted a different colour.

The standing building survey took place after the buildings had been vacated, and many internal features, such as fireplaces, doors and timber sash windows, had been removed. Each house had been extensively altered by generations of tenants and owners, but by examining and recording the features in each, and by studying photographs held by the Roseberry Place Residents' Association, it is possible to reconstruct the terrace's original appearance and understand the subsequent changes. The rooms on the ground floor had moulded plaster cornices and the rear windows originally had internal folding panelled timber shutters. The rooms on the upper

floor were rather more plain, and an extension had been constructed at the rear of each of the houses in the terrace, containing a kitchen and bathroom; these probably replaced earlier privies and outbuildings which were demolished when the NLR was constructed and later expanded. Examination of census returns from the 19th century shows that the houses were initially occupied by families of various occupations, but, as the railways expanded, a greater number of people employed by the NLR, and their families, are recorded as living in 5–13 Roseberry Place. The 1911 census shows that most of the houses were occupied by single families whose heads worked as railway inspectors, porters and signalmen. No. 5 Roseberry Place was occupied by two families: George Chapman, who worked as a signalman, and his wife, son, three daughters and a lodger; and Henry Winter, a warehouseman, and his wife and 7-month-old son William.

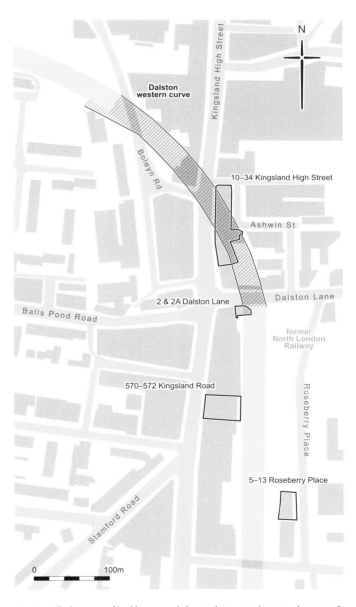

Fig 105 Starling's map of Hackney of 1831 (scale 1:3340)

Fig 106 The locations of buildings recorded in Dalston, in relation to the route of the North London Railway (scale 1:5000)

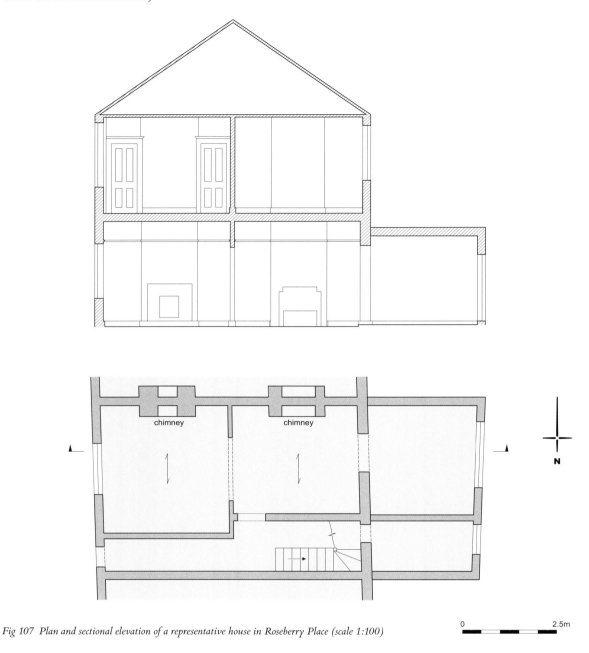

Fig 107 Plan and sectional elevation of a representative house in Roseberry Place (scale 1:100)

0   2.5m

6.2 The construction of the North London Railway

Founded after the initial railway mania of the 1840s, when schemes for the construction of mainlines connecting the metropolitan centres of the country abounded, the NLR, completed in 1850, was intended to link the various lines serving the railway termini of north London to the East India Docks, to the west of the mouth of the River Lea, and the West India Docks at the northern end of the Isle of Dogs, facilitating the transfer of goods, rather than passengers, between the railway lines. The company which constructed and ran the railway was known as the East and West India Docks and Birmingham Junction Railway until 1853, when it changed its name to the more succinct 'North London Railway'.

Initially trains ran from Camden Town in the north to Poplar in the east, passing through Dalston, where a station (Dalston Kingsland) opened in Kingsland High Street in 1850 (Fig 108). From Poplar trains ran via the London and Blackwall Railway to the East and West India Docks; a connection at Bow allowed trains to also run to Fenchurch Street on the eastern side of the City of London. This route was rather circuitous, so in 1861 the North London Railway (City Branch) Act was passed, enabling the construction of a new branch line with a triangular junction and a station at Dalston, a terminus at Broad Street on the north-eastern edge of the City of London, and an intermediate station in Shoreditch at the junction of Old Street and Shoreditch High Street (and not to be confused with the earlier Shoreditch terminus of the Eastern Counties Railway, 250m to the south, or the slightly later Shoreditch station of the East London Railway). The line opened in 1865, and an

Fig 108 The former Dalston Kingsland railway station in the early 20th century, looking north-west (NLR, Laurie Ward collection, box 2, album 9, 1925/6, National Railway Museum/SSPL)

additional intermediate station was opened at Lee Street in Haggerston in 1867.

Dalston Junction station contained six platforms, connected by two footbridges, with canopied shelters supported by cast iron columns. The main entrance to the station was situated on the southern side of Dalston Lane, but an additional ticket office was located on the western side of Roseberry Place. The station forecourt contained a receiving office for parcels, as well as shops, which in 1915 were let out to an estate agents and tobacconist.

6.3 Excavation at Lee Street

Just as the construction of the Braithwaite viaduct (Chapter 4.3) more than 20 years before had displaced people along with their homes and businesses, the construction of the NLR branch line from Dalston Junction to Broad Street station also required the demolition of homes and the removal of those who lived in them. The line's viaduct ran parallel with the eastern side of Kingsland Road, and so cut across Lee Street at a right angle, necessitating the demolition of Nos 3–7 which had been standing for not much more than 20 years. The excavation of evaluation trenches on the former rear plots of 3–7 Lee Street (Fig 109) has afforded an insight into life in Haggerston immediately prior to the construction of the NLR.

Historic maps show that Lee Street was not constructed until the period between 1841 (the street does not appear in the

census of that year) and 1851. Before the 19th century the site stood within open fields (Fig 110), on an estate leased by Mr Lee, Esq (HAD, V2). A map of 1775 does not show any

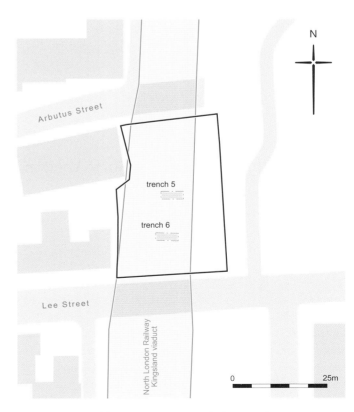

Fig 109 Location of the Lee Street excavation (scale: 1:1000)

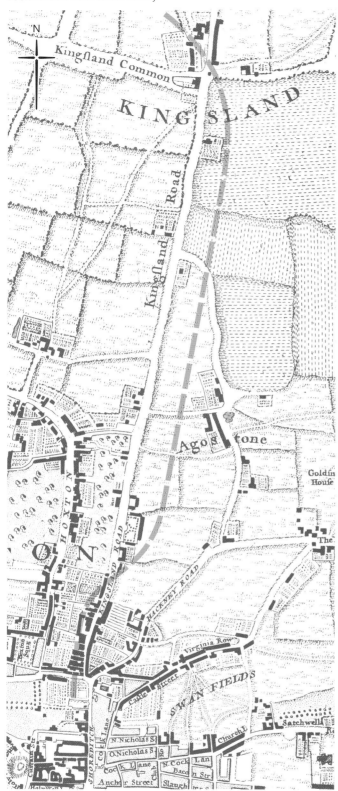

Fig 110 The course of Lee Street projected on John Rocque's map of London of 1746

The suburban area gradually developed along the Kingsland Road, and during the 19th century slowly spread outwards into the open fields. The construction of the Regent's Canal and various docks along its route provided a great stimulus for both industrial and domestic development in the adjacent areas. The need for workers and businesses to maintain the growing number of new inhabitants presented the opportunity for landowners of sizeable estates to speculate and build new housing, as can be seen in the names of streets and housing estates in the area; it is likely that Lee Street memorialised the man who leased the estate (LMA, DC/ED/009).

The census returns indicate that for the most part each house in Lee Street was home to a single family, generally comprising between four and seven individuals. In 1851, 4 Lee Street was occupied by a single family comprising the father, mother, three daughters, one son and a servant. No. 6, on the other hand, was occupied by three separate families, two of three people, and one of two; this had changed little by 1861. Only two names of people living in Lee Street could be identified in both the 1851 and 1861 censuses, Charlotte Horne and Joseph White, indicating a high level of mobility among the street's residents (though this is not particularly unusual for the period), with people migrating into London from the surrounding countryside, and moving about within the city and its suburbs. The poorer families and individuals were particularly disadvantaged by transience, moving from one dwelling to another as financial and occupational circumstances fluctuated as a result of illness or unemployment. In 1851 the majority of the inhabitants of Lee Street were born outside London, with just under one third of inhabitants being recorded as born in the parish of Shoreditch. The professions specified in the census records reveal that the houses were occupied by a mixture of tradespeople and the semi-clerical, ranging from a handloom weaver of rugs and a goldbeater to a Returning Officer and a professor of languages. The professions listed indicate that the area was inhabited by families that floated between the upper levels of the lower classes and the lower and middle levels of the middle classes.

A larger swathe of land and properties was purchased by the North London Railway Company than was needed for the construction of the line, and the pamphlet which accompanied the sale of unwanted property after the construction of the railway (HAD, M3560) goes some way towards indicating the size and appearance of the demolished properties of 3–7 Lee Street. The left-over properties, namely 1, 2, 8 and 9 Lee Street, were described in the sale pamphlet as six-roomed houses each with a water-closet and garden, with a rental value of between £48 and £54 per year, and it is likely that these houses were similar to Nos 3–7. No. 10 was a house and beer shop, the Lord Clyde, with a rent of £94 per year. On Booth's *Descriptive map of London poverty* of 1889 (Chapter 4.7), the houses of Lee Street were coloured purple, indicating that the occupants were classified as 'Mixed – Some comfortable, others poor'.

The excavation of two evaluation trenches (Fig 111) under an arch of the disused railway viaduct adjacent to Lee Street, in advance of the construction of the new Haggerston station,

buildings, but does indicate that the parish boundary and the line of what would become Acton (now Arbutus) Road in part followed the line of an ancient stream that had been canalised by the time Stanford's map of 1862 was published (LMA, DC/ED/009).

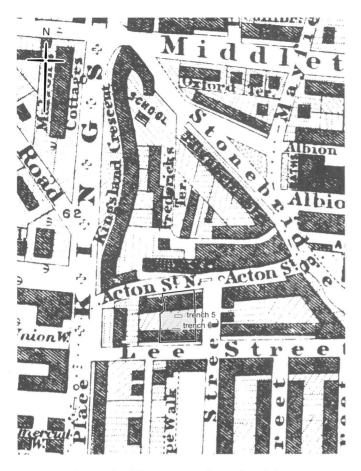

Fig 111 Trenches 5 and 6 of the Lee Street evaluation (site F) shown on Stanford's map of London of 1862 (scale 1:4000)

revealed a circular brick-lined cesspit (F[8]) in trench 5, below the later granite sett surface which was installed underneath the arch. The backfill of the cesspit consisted of a mixture of black silt, white mortar fragments, brick rubble and decayed wood (probably from the associated privy structure), along with rubbish deposited on the cusp of the 1860s comprising pottery, glass, clay tobacco pipes and the remains of a sewer pipe. While the cesspit contained broken pottery from incremental house and yard clearances, the bulk of the assemblage from the backfilling of the cesspit can be linked to the compulsory purchases and demolition of 3–7 Lee Street in advance of the construction of the railway.

What cannot be determined, however, is who was responsible for the disposal of the finds from the cesspit; whether the objects left behind in 3–7 Lee Street were gathered up and thrown into the cesspit immediately prior to demolition by NLR workers, or whether the disposal of objects represented a final act of abandonment and closure by the inhabitants of a single house. One glass spirit flask (<G4>, Fig 113) was certainly local to the site, originating from the Black Bull public house at 20 Hertford Place in Haggerston. The similarly dated glass, ceramics and clay pipes discarded in this feature are all good examples of the sorts of 'proper dry rubbish' preferred for filling in holes in the ground during the Victorian period (Jeffries 2006, 275), and the feature served as a

convenient receptacle in which to discard a range of unwanted items before moving.

The cesspit contained objects that were characteristic of mid 19th-century life, with a few ceramic vessels associated with the consumption of food and drink, including a 'Pratt ware' pot lid (Savage and Newman 2000, 230) from the 1860s (<P27>, Fig 112). This lid, with three-colour transfer-printed decoration (TPW5), was used for the 'Strasbourg' range of speciality pastes made by the company Crosse and Blackwell; it depicts a view of this French city from the River Ill, and the bottom outside edge reads '…bourg prise du port'. Another lid in refined whiteware with black transfer-printed decoration (TPW3) would also have been used to seal a jar containing conserves, preserves or pastes. Both lids represent a material response to the industrialised improvements being made in food preservation, before the advent of refrigeration. A yellow ware (YELL) 'London'-shape bowl with mocha decoration (Goodwin and Barker 2009, figs 31–2, 15) is of a ubiquitous type, common in London assemblages from the 1830s onwards, and was used for the consumption of sloppy foods. A coffee can in refined white earthenware with industrial slip decoration (REFW SLIP) with a moulded phoenix was also found (<P28>, Fig 112), and a cream jug (<P29>, Fig 112) and mug (<P30>, Fig 112) are examples of transfer-printed refined whitewares with 'flow blue' decoration (TPW FLOW; ibid, 61; Brooks 2005, 39–40); both were purchases made after the mid 1830s and demonstrate an apparent desire to obtain aesthetically similar wares.

Performing different functions within this Lee Street property were two identical small-sized brown-glazed stoneware (ENGS) bottles (<P31> and <P32>, Fig 112), probably London-made, which may have functioned as small ink bottles (Green 1999, fig 138, no. 412). Alternatively they may have been miniatures, fitting well with the 'nursery' mug (<P33>, Fig 112) in refined whiteware with blue transfer-printed stipple and line decoration (TPW2). The print depicts an image of two boys straddling a makeshift seesaw, reflecting the social lives of children who, according to the census returns for 1851, represented 55% of the occupants of Lee Street. The cup is just one example of the staggering quantity of crockery bearing endearing and sentimental images of children at play during the Victorian period (cf Jeffries et al 2009; Brighton 2001), a case of manufacturing tapping into the increasingly emotive and romantic notions that middle class Victorians began to attach to childhood.

The mug and its associations stand in stark contrast to a material trace of arguably the main vice of the period, drink (Blackmore and Egan 2009). It was an affliction that social reformers and journalists particularly attributed to the masses of the East End, manifested in the establishment of the alcohol-free entertainments of the 'Tee-To-Tum Tea Stores' in Kingsland High Street. Two complete pale green moulded glass spirit flasks were found discarded in the pit at site F. The first (<G4>, Fig 113), an oval-shaped flask (height 170mm), bears an integrally moulded, oval proprietorial seal reading J.TILLEY / WATER AND SPIRIT MERCH.T / BLACK / BULL / HAGGERSTONE. It is likely that the bottle originated from

Fig 112 Ceramic finds from cesspit fill F[8]: refined whiteware pot lid <P27> with polychrome transfer-printed (TPW5) decoration depicting the French city of Strasbourg; refined white earthenware with industrial slip decoration (REFW SLIP) coffee can <P28>; transfer-printed whiteware with 'flow blue' decoration (TPW FLOW) cream jug <P29> and mug <P30>; English stoneware (ENGS) bottles <P31> and <P32>; refined white earthenware nursery mug <P33> with blue transfer-printed decoration (TPW2) (scale c 1:2 except <P27> at 1:1)

the Black Bull, at 20 Hertford Place, and a short-lived licencee J (Joseph) Tilley who is listed here in 1855–6 only (in the 56th and 57th London Post Office street and trade directory: HAD). The second spirit flask (<G5>, Fig 113) is sub-octagonal (height *c* 140mm), rectangular-shaped with flat chamfers and larger flat faces possibly for paper labels, though there is a moulded 'R' at the top of one of these areas. Both flasks have mineral-shaped rims. The consumption of spirits contrasts with the function of the remaining two glass bottles discarded here, which held patent medicines. These two aqua-coloured moulded glass bottles (<G6> and <G7>, Fig 113) are round-sectioned vessels with packer rim finish, and are both graduated for gauging the amount of the contents left, or for dispensation, with three regularly spaced horizontal dosage lines.

Completing the small but revealing amount of rubbish discarded in the cesspit was a group of four clay tobacco pipe bowls dated to *c* 1860–80, three of which are decorated and bear makers' marks (Grey 2009c). The first pipe (<CP7>) is of a

London type dated 1840–80 and decorated with leaves running down the seams at the front and back of the bowl, and is marked with a shield moulded in relief on the sides of the spur; this motif is paralleled on a pipe from the Tower of London moat (Higgins 2004, no. 42). Subtle decorative differences from the Tower of London pipe – here the leaves alternate with spikes – suggest an earlier date within the date range for that type. On the Lee Street pipe the leaves are closely spaced and continuous, suggesting a date after 1860. Pipe <CP8>, a London type dated 1850–1910, is a Victorian novelty pipe decorated with vertical ribbing below swags on the bowl. The third and fourth pipes are marked with initials, although the identity of the pipe makers could not be confirmed: <CP9> is marked WW in relief on the sides of the spur, and pipe <CP10> is marked WD in relief along the sides of the stem. The latter pipe is elaborately decorated with a rose and thistle at the top of the bowl, vertical ribbing below, and leaves running along the seams of the stem where the maker's mark is located.

Fig 113 Glass finds from cesspit fill F[8]: pale green oval-shaped spirit flask with seal <G4> and rectangular spirit flask with flat chamfers <G5>; two pale aqua-coloured medicine bottles with graduated dosage lines <G6> and <G7> (scale c 1:2, details 1:1)

An element of wastefulness, representing the greater number of mass-produced goods, and perhaps the relative affluence of the residents, can be detected in the assemblage, with usable glass medicine and spirit bottles being considered just as valueless as the broken pottery found alongside them.

6.4 The railways arrive

Stanford's map of London of 1862 (Fig 114) shows the impact that the arrival of the railways had on Dalston. The opening of the North London Railway from Camden Town to Poplar, and of Dalston Kingsland station, in 1850 had made the area more attractive for commuters to the city. The village had developed further, and more streets of smaller terraced houses, such as Roseberry Place, had been built on what was formerly open land. There were still large parts of Dalston and Kingsland that had not been developed, however; the NLR was intended to connect the eastern docks with the trains for the north at Camden, and took a circuitous route into the City via Bow.

The North London Railway (City Branch) Act of 1861 (above, 6.2) enabled the construction of a spur from Dalston Lane, where a new station would be built, to a new terminus at Broad Street. The new spur was connected to the existing line by way of two curves; the western curve crossed below Kingsland High Street and met with the earlier line at a point to the west of Dalston Kingsland station, which subsequently closed. In 1866–7 the NLR sought additional powers, which were granted, to widen the railway; it appears that the railway had proved to be more popular than originally anticipated. Widening the railway would require the demolition and alteration of further buildings on the eastern side of Kingsland High Street.

Broad Street station and the viaducts on which the railway

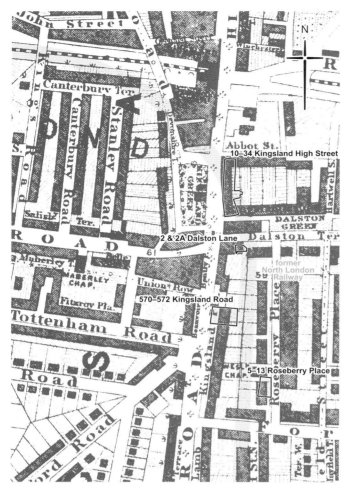

Abbot St.
10—34 Kingsland High Street

2 & 2A Dalston Lane

former
North London
Railway

570—572 Kingsland Road

5—13 Roseberry Place

Fig 114 The route of the North London Railway through Dalston, with the building recording locations, shown on Stanford's map of London of 1862 (scale 1:4000)

was carried were shared with another company, the London and North Western Railway. Although the Broad Street terminus was intended to serve passengers commuting to the City from London's western, northern and eastern suburbs, goods traffic was also an important part of the business; in 1868 a goods station was opened by the LNWR immediately to the west of the passenger station, with a depot at ground level and a lift to transport wagons from the top of the viaduct to the arches underneath.

The branch line from Dalston Junction to Broad Street was carried on the Holywell and Kingsland viaducts, with a bridge carrying the railway over Shoreditch High Street. On the approach to Dalston, the railway entered a cutting, and would have been divided into two as the lines passed into the two underground 'curves', one carrying trains to the west and the other to the east.

Like the earlier Braithwaite viaduct of the Eastern Counties Railway, the viaducts and brick-lined cutting of the NLR were constructed to carry railway lines through the heavily built-up areas of east London and over the Regent's Canal with the minimum of impact on the surrounding streets. The NLR avoided road crossings at street level, which would have been

impractical in busy streets, and viaducts had the benefit of incorporating vaults, which could be let out to businesses and thereby raise additional revenue for the railway company. Further to the east, the arches of the London and Blackwall Railway, which opened in 1840, were infilled in places with houses, and the curate of St George-in-the-East in Poplar established a school underneath three of the arches. There is no evidence that the NLR viaducts were used for such purposes, however. Viaducts were expensive to build, but obtaining the land on which to build a railway was also costly; appropriation of land was enabled by Act of Parliament, which mandated the payment by the railway company of compensation to the previous landowners but not necessarily, at this time, to the occupiers and tenants, even though the redevelopment often entailed the demolition of houses and shops and the removal of their occupants. A viaduct had a smaller footprint than an earthen embankment, and so reduced the amount of land that would have to be compulsorily purchased (Hughes 1979, 140); it would also be passable in places, maintaining – in theory at least – existing patterns of movement through the streets.

In 1867, only two years after the NLR branch line from Dalston Junction to Broad Street had opened, it was proposed that it should be widened to accommodate additional traffic. The construction work was carried out on the western side of the railway line in 1874; several bridges were reconstructed at this time, including that carrying the Holywell viaduct over the entrance to a yard on the eastern side of King John Court. During the widening of the Holywell viaduct, human remains from the priory which stood on the site were found and 'reburied, or bricked up in the pocket-arches of the bridge in King John's Court' (Hudson 1896–7, 471). No such remains were recorded during the watching brief of the demolition of the bridge.

The Holywell viaduct runs approximately south to north from the northern side of Holywell Street (formerly Holywell Lane) to Old Street, before bearing north-north-east to meet Kingsland Road (the A10) on the former line of the Roman Ermine Street. The NLR was carried over the Kingsland Road from 1874 on a 'Pratt truss' bridge, constructed of riveted wrought iron plate beams; this bridge still stands, and forms part of the extended East London line (Fig 115). Each of this kind of bridge's trusses comprises top and bottom rails (or chords) connected by a series of vertical compression members and diagonal tension members (Morriss 2003, 92); the bridge deck is tied to the lower chords.

Railway arches were leased by local businesses and used as warehouses, workshops and stabling, such as those under the Holywell viaduct in Reliance Square (Fig 116). The Post Office directory for 1895 (HAD) indicates that some of the arches were used by Wilkinson and Son, timber merchants, who had a large timber yard and offices at 186 Shoreditch High Street. Further north, the Gas Light and Coke Company leased a number of railway arches in the Kingsland viaduct adjacent to their gasworks in Laburnam Street, on the southern side of the Regent's Canal in Haggerston; the arches were used for storerooms, workshops and offices, and in 1879 the company planned to erect a gas testing house and other buildings on the

Fig 115 *The North London Railway crossing the Kingsland Road in 1961, looking north towards Hoxton and Dalston (HAD, HAP7432, image courtesy of London Borough of Hackney Archives)*

Fig 116 *The railway arch and tenements of Reliance Square, Shoreditch, in 1898, looking east (City of London, London Metropolitan Archives, SC/PHL/01/361)*

strip of land on the eastern side of the viaduct, which had been reserved for use as a roadway by way of an easement.

The Kingsland viaduct runs north-north-east from the eastern side of Kingsland Road to Cremer Street (formerly Thomas Street) before bearing north as far as Middleton Road. To the north of Middleton Road the railway line entered a cutting, to accommodate the rise in ground level towards Dalston and so maintain a workable gradient for the steam engines, and also to allow trains to pass below the centre of Dalston. The construction of the junction with the existing NLR line from Bow to Kew required the western and eastern curves to be built within a cutting, so that the new branch line could merge with the existing railway line.

The profile of a railway cutting depended largely on the geology of the ground encountered, and whether the railway passed through an urban or a rural area; engineers had to ensure that material did not slip down the sides of the cutting on to the track. Where a cutting was made through stone, its sides could be steep, but where a railway line was cut through clay, sand or gravel, as at Dalston, the unreliable nature of the ground necessitated a shallow slope to the sides of the cutting. The price of land in London, like other urban areas throughout the country, was so great, and the politics of removing large numbers of buildings and people so problematic, however, that a financial saving could be made by constructing a narrow cutting lined with vertical brick walls (Morriss 2003, 40), and just such a method of construction was used on the NLR. The narrow width of the cutting required refuge arches to be incorporated into the fabric of the yellow stock brick walls, where railway workers could stand safely while a train passed.

The cutting walls of Dalston western curve were thicker at their base, with projecting ledges at the same level as the bridge decks, and had been extensively repaired and rebuilt, perhaps after sustaining bomb damage during the Second World War. Like the Kingsland and Holywell viaducts to the south, the railway cutting was widened on its western side in 1874 and the western cutting walls were rebuilt. The former western piers of the overbridges were retained and new track beds were laid between them and the new cutting walls, resulting in the overbridges of Dalston Lane, the private road leading to the Kingsland public house, Boleyn Road and the covered way having room for two sets of tracks on the wider, original course of the western curve, and space for a single track in the widened section.

The covered way was constructed in a similar manner to the other bridges, with riveted wrought iron plate and steel beams supporting intermediate brick jack-arches. The beams were carried on brick piers, which supported the road and several buildings in Kingsland High Street. Parts of the deck in Kingsland High Street were rebuilt in 1904 with steel beams and concrete cast *in situ*; the bridge had to be strengthened in order to carry trams for the London County Council (LCC), and two of the girders were broken and needed replacing. The provision of electric trams ironically led to the decline of the NLR. A number of businesses in Kingsland High Street received compensation for the disruption caused by the bridge

repair works (LMA, LCC/PP/BR/088).

Like other suburban passenger railways, the NLR also played a role in the transportation of goods. A goods station was constructed on the southern side of Pearson Street, on the former site of houses which stood on the western side of Parker Street (later renamed Ormsby Street) and Nichol's Square. The goods station was first shown on the 2nd edition Ordnance Survey map of 1894–6. The Post Office directory of 1916 (HAD) lists Mr F A Sargent as superintendent of the salvage office which was based there.

At its peak, just before 1900, Broad Street had become the third busiest railway station in London for passengers, after Liverpool Street and Victoria. From the beginning of the 20th century, however, Broad Street station went into severe decline, mainly because of competition from the London Underground and the tramways, which were expanding out into the suburbs. The NLR merged with the LNWR in 1909, and shortly afterwards the decision was made to electrify the lines; the work was carried out in 1916, and used a four-rail system similar to that used on the underground (Robbins 1967, 11). At this time an electricity substation adjacent to the railway line in Dalston was installed to convert alternating current to direct current.

6.5 The expansion of Dalston

The 1st edition Ordnance Survey map of 1870 (Fig 117) shows that there had been further intensive development of the area. In order to construct Dalston Junction station and the line to Broad Street, a terrace on the southern side of Dalston Lane had to be demolished. The railway line was constructed largely over the rear gardens of properties fronting the eastern side of Kingsland Road, although some properties in Roseberry Place were demolished and the northern end of the road was realigned. The construction of Dalston western curve, the covered way which connected the spur to Broad Street with the original NLR line to the north, involved the demolition of properties on the northern side of Dalston Lane and both sides of Kingsland High Street. A public house (the King's Arms) and a row of shops to the north appear to have been rebuilt, although a plot of land on the western side of the road was still vacant. The land to the north of the western end of Dalston Lane came to be largely industrial in use after the construction of the Broad Street branch of the NLR, the two curves connecting it with the earlier mainline and an adjacent coal depot.

Charles Booth's *Descriptive map of London poverty* of 1889 (Chapter 4.7; Fig 118) depicts Dalston as being overwhelmingly occupied by middle-class (red) and financially comfortable (pink) households. Some areas, namely those sandwiched between the various railway lines, Dalston Lane and Kingsland High Street, were occupied by poor families (light blue), earning between 18s and 21s a week, and very poor families

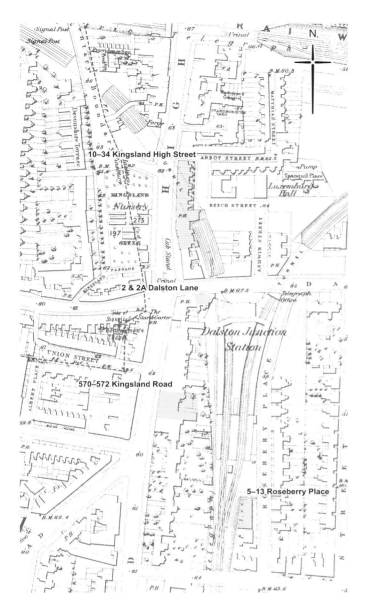

Fig 117 The route of the North London Railway through Dalston, shown on the 1st edition Ordnance Survey 25in to the mile map of 1870 (scale 1:2250)

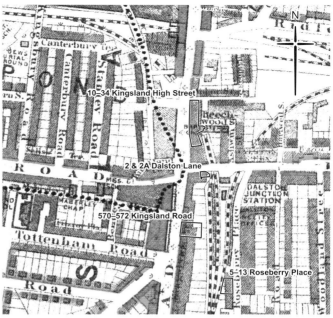

Fig 118 An extract from Charles Booth's Descriptive map of London poverty *of 1889, showing Dalston*

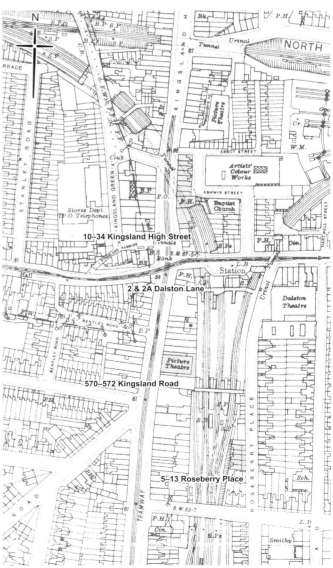

(dark blue) engaged only in casual labour.

The 3rd edition Ordnance Survey map of 1916 (Fig 119) shows that the NLR line had been widened according to the plans laid out in 1866–7 and had taken up more of the rear gardens of properties in Kingsland Road. Bridges had been widened, new cutting walls built and an additional single-track tunnel had been constructed to the west of the covered way below Kingsland High Street. Again, this necessitated the demolition of buildings in the High Street, and the King's Arms public house appears to have been partially rebuilt at this time. The plot of land on the western side of the High Street, on the corner with Boleyn Road, had been developed by this time.

Fig 119 The route of the North London Railway through Dalston, shown on the 3rd edition Ordnance Survey 25in to the mile map of 1916 (scale 1:2534)

The Post Office street directories of the late 19th and early 20th centuries bear witness to the diversity of businesses attracted to the, by now, thriving commercial heart of Dalston, including butchers, tailors, umbrella makers and – as part of a movement to counter the large number of public houses in 19th-century London – the Tee-To-Tum Tea Stores, a teetotal drinking establishment.

Nos 2 and 2A Dalston Lane

No. 2 Dalston Lane (Fig 120; Fig 121) was a three-storey building with a basement on the southern side of Dalston Lane, constructed of yellow stock brick at some point between 1870 and 1894, when it is first depicted on the 1st edition Ordnance Survey map. A single-storey shop, 2A Dalston Lane, appears to have been contemporary with it. The 1881 census lists tobacconist Henry Pye, his wife Ann, children Augustus and Edith, and servant Lydia Gibbs as residing in the building. The northern and eastern external walls of the building faced on to Dalston Lane, and were well decorated, with stone window dressings, dentilled cornices and blind windows in the eastern elevation; the slate roof was obscured behind a brick parapet. The south-facing external wall, which looked out on to the railway cutting, was rather plainer, and a small three-storey extension containing lavatories had been built on this side.

No. 2 Dalston Lane had been purpose-built as a shop; the last occupant of the ground floor and basement was a shoe-

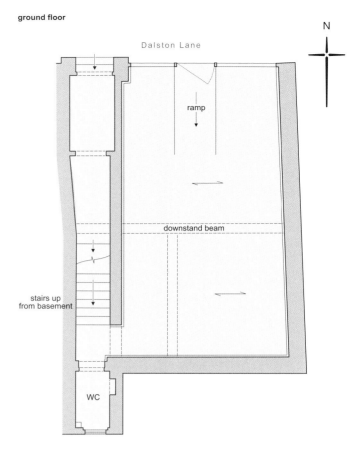

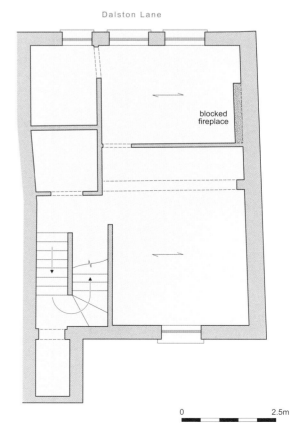

Fig 120 The exterior of 2 Dalston Lane, looking south

Fig 121 Plans of the ground floor and first floor of 2 Dalston Lane (scale 1:100)

shop, but it had previously been used as a branch of Lockhart's refreshment rooms in the late 19th and early 20th centuries, being ideally located adjacent to the railway station. The upper floors had their own separate entrance on the western side of the building; the entrance hall was separated from the shop by a thin timber stud wall, which had reused timber panels with late 19th-century advertising posters and bills still adhering to them. A staircase at the rear of the ground floor shop led to the basement, which had an external door in its southern wall that appears to have led to one of the platforms of Dalston Junction station; perhaps the basement served as platform-level refreshment rooms for travellers who had already purchased their tickets, or facilitated stock deliveries by train.

The first and second floors had latterly been used as offices by a minicab firm and solicitors respectively, but were built for use as a dwelling, probably for the tenant of the ground-floor shop and basement. An extension was added to the rear of the building in the late 19th century to accommodate lavatories, accessed from the landings at the rear of the ground floor, between the ground and first floors and between the first and second floors.

No. 2A Dalston Lane was constructed at the same time as 2 Dalston Lane as a single-storey shop, having large curving plate glass windows with tall transom lights above stallrisers, and a recessed lobby. The building, constructed of stock brick with a flat roof, had a small stockroom and a yard with an outbuilding which was concealed behind the remnant of the station facade in Dalston Lane.

Nos 10–16 Kingsland High Street

Nos 10–16 Kingsland High Street were constructed at some point between 1870 and 1894; the earlier buildings on the site were demolished when the covered way was widened. The Post Office street directory of 1882 (HAD) indicates that No. 10 was the premises of Thomas Powles, an umbrella maker. No. 12 was occupied by John Thomas, a grocer, and a post office and savings bank also operated from the premises. Cheesemonger Henry Ritchings and butchers Barrett and Slater had premises at Nos 14 and 16 respectively. The census of 1881 suggests that none of these buildings were used as residences, however, as none of these four addresses are listed in the census returns. It is possible that the occupants were simply absent on the day the census was taken, but equally the rooms on the upper floors, intended for use as residences, may have served as storage. By 1899, No. 12 had been taken over by Mr P G Buchanan, who had set up there one of seven branches of the 'Tee-To-Tum', a teetotal drinking and dining establishment which was a spin-off from the University Club at Oxford House, a religious and educational institute in Cambridge Road, Bethnal Green. Oxford House was established by graduates of Oxford University and hosted a library and lectures for its one thousand members. In 1886 Oxford House founded the Federation of Working Men's Clubs, in order to oversee the provision of recreation, education and 'non-intoxicant refreshment' (*VCH* 1998, 147–50). The University Club was just one of a number of cultural institutions established by Oxford House for the betterment of the East End's poor at the end of the 19th century; the Webbe Institute for Working Boys opened in 1888 in Bethnal Green Road, was financed by friends of H B Webbe, a New College man and cricketer, and provided a gymnasium, games and a band. The staff and pupils of other wealthy educational institutions also established clubs and societies for the East End's poor; Repton Boxing Club, which has trained generations of internationally renowned sportsmen, grew out of Repton Boys' Club, established in 1884 by the Derbyshire public school, and the Eton Mission in Hackney Wick was established by Eton College for the religious wellbeing of the poor (*VCH* 1995, 68–70).

The terrace of four three-storey purpose-built shops with basements and attics was constructed of brick with slate roofs, and the buildings had been extensively altered internally. The rear elevation was largely rebuilt and the shop fronts updated to keep up with fashion and changing use, although remnants of pilasters and consoles from the shop fronts remained at ground-floor level. The first floor of 10 Kingsland High Street in particular showed evidence of having been rebuilt; the consoles of a large plate glass window on the first floor remained, the window having been replaced by two smaller windows with concrete lintels to match those belonging to Nos 12–16, probably when the upper floors of the building were converted for use as two flats in 1998 (www.hackney.gov.uk, planning application no. SOUTH/150/98/FP).

The ground-floor shops had been altered by the addition of internal partition walls; in 12 Kingsland High Street, which was occupied by a nail bar, a partition wall separated the treatment area from the storage room at the rear, and at No. 16 the ground-floor shop was divided by a partition wall into a Chinese herbal remedy shop and an outlet for the sale of phone cards. The upper floors of 12–16 Kingsland High Street were significantly altered when the buildings were converted to accommodate eight flats in 1995 (www.hackney.gov.uk, planning application no. SOUTH/366/95/FP); this work removed the chimney breasts and fireplaces from the building, along with early windows and internal fixtures and fittings, in order to produce a building fit for multiple occupancy. Extensions were constructed over the rear yards during the 20th century, increasing the size of the retail premises; the original rear wall of 14 Kingsland High Street, along with the window and door openings which would have opened on to the yard, was maintained.

The King's Arms public house, 18 Kingsland High Street

The King's Arms public house (Fig 122; Fig 123) was constructed in at least two phases; the pub was first built after the completion of the Dalston western curve in 1865, and subsequently extended from Kingsland High Street to Ashwin Street. The front part of the building was demolished in order to widen the covered way of Dalston western curve, and was rebuilt in the 1870s. In 1881 the publican of the King's Arms was widow Margaret Rich, assisted by her three daughters Kate,

Fig 122 The exterior of the King's Arms public house, looking east

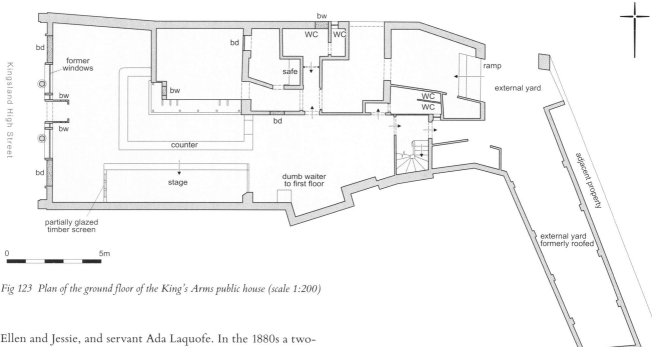

Fig 123 Plan of the ground floor of the King's Arms public house (scale 1:200)

Ellen and Jessie, and servant Ada Laquofe. In the 1880s a two-storey, stock brick extension with a flat roof was added, which contained a staircase to the first floor. The census of 1901 lists a different publican, Henry Baynes, along with a housekeeper, her son, and six servants all working in the pub.

The King's Arms public house was constructed of brick, covered with render at the rear, and had white-painted stucco dressings to the roof parapet, which concealed the pitched slate roof, and first-floor windows of the main facade in Kingsland High Street; in front of these windows, scrolled wrought iron

railings would have contained window boxes with floral displays. The ground floor was dominated by the granite and timber shop front, the timber fascia of which was supported by granite pillars and pilasters with decorated consoles.

The fascia was surmounted by a broken pediment which enclosed the number '18'. The shop front contained three door openings, which probably originally gave access to the public bar, saloon and perhaps an off-licence area. The ground floor of the King's Arms comprised the large, open bar space including a raised stage area for live music bands. The bar area would have originally been further subdivided into the public bar, saloon and rear service rooms. The northern side of the ground floor contained an office, with a safe set into a concrete block, public lavatories, and storage rooms for beer barrels and spirits; the building's position over the covered way precluded the presence of a cellar, other than a small area at the western end of the building, adjacent to Kingsland High Street. Deliveries were made to the storage rooms via the pub's rear entrance in Ashwin Street. The staircase to the first floor was located at the rear of the building, in a later extension, and it may have originally been located more centrally within the building.

The first floor of the building suggested something of the original layout; this floor was arranged on two levels, with the rear (older) part of the building being at a lower level than the front portion, which had been rebuilt in the 1870s. A corridor extended from the staircase at the rear of the building along an east–west axis, with rooms leading off that had been used as the living quarters for the publican and staff. The first floor had been altered, but the rooms would have had ornate fireplaces and ceiling cornices. The kitchen was located in the rear, older portion of the building, and a dumb waiter would have delivered meals to the ground floor. After the closure of the pub in 2008 the building was used by squatters.

The storage rooms at the rear of the King's Arms were accessed via doors in the northern elevation of the building, on Ashwin Street, and the pavement to the north of the doors had been altered by the addition of large granite slabs which acted as a 'barrel-run' into the storage room for beer deliveries. The rear yard of the King's Arms extended southwards from Ashwin Street and was located on the eastern side of the Dalston western curve cutting. The yard was surrounded by brick walls with projecting buttresses which formerly supported a sloping roof, although this had been removed by the time of the survey.

Nos 20–34 Kingsland High Street

Nos 20–34 Kingsland High Street were originally constructed between 1865 and 1870, after earlier buildings on the site were demolished in order to construct the covered way of Dalston western curve. The widening of the latter in the 1870s necessitated the demolition and reconstruction of 20–24 Kingsland High Street. The row of shops was constructed of brick, with flat roofs supported by riveted and bolted wrought iron plate beams. Originally all the buildings were of one storey, as this placed less of a load on the bridge deck structure, although two of the girders which carried the bridge deck of Kingsland High Street still failed and had to be replaced in 1904.

Each shop had a rear yard with an outbuilding, but these were gradually infilled and a two-storey extension was added to the rear of 28–30 Kingsland High Street. A staircase was inserted against the internal face of the northern wall of the building, which gave access to the first floor, situated at the rear of the building. The rear of the ground floor was originally illuminated by a stained glass window which took up the majority of the space in the eastern rear wall, although by the time of the survey the internal face of the window was covered by plasterboard. The first floor contained a north–south aligned corridor, at the head of the stairs, which gave access to a storage cupboard and three rooms, used as an office and storage room, a kitchen and a lavatory.

The interior of the ground floor of each shop was very plain, allowing shopkeepers to adapt their premises, such as installing sinks and additional lighting for the nail parlour at 12 Kingsland High Street, or adding racks for hanging clothing at No. 34 (Fig 124). The original shop fronts had been replaced with plate glass windows which extended across the width of each one, protected out of hours by steel rolling shutters and grilles, and with internally lit plastic box signs, although some fascia consoles and the clock erected by Skeggs Jewellers above 28–30 Kingsland High Street remained.

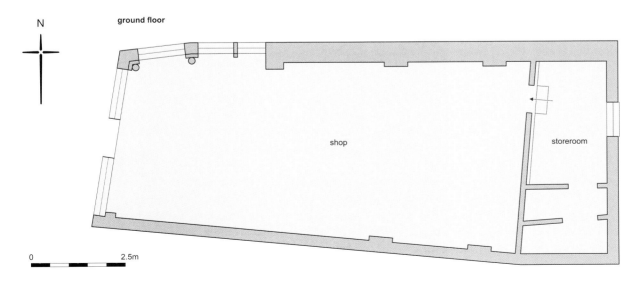

Fig 124 Plan of the ground floor of 34 Kingsland High Street (scale 1:100)

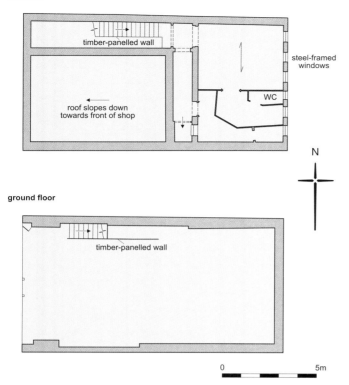

first floor

timber-panelled wall

steel-framed windows

WC

roof slopes down towards front of shop

N

ground floor

timber-panelled wall

0   5m

Fig 125 Plans of the ground floor and first floor of 28–30 Kingsland High Street (scale 1:200)

The mostly single-storey shops with rear storage rooms were not suitable for residential use and so do not appear in census returns, with the exception of 28–30 Kingsland High Street, the premises of Charles and Arthur Skeggs, jewellers (Fig 125). A two-storey extension was added to the rear of the building at the end of the 19th century, and the census returns of 1881 and 1901 indicate that a presence was maintained within the building overnight, presumably to act as on-site security. In 1881 Edward Paternoster, a 46-year-old jewellers' porter, and William Reed, a 20-year-old jewellers' assistant, were residing in the building; by the time of the 1901 census this role was carried out by John Lumer, a jewellers' packer.

Entertainment in Dalston

The late 19th and early 20th centuries saw Dalston's expansion as a commercial and entertainment centre, including several pubs and cinemas. The Ordnance Survey map published in 1916 shows no fewer than five cinemas and theatres and 13 public houses within a 300m radius of Dalston Junction station (Fig 126), and there were many more restaurants and tea rooms not indicated on maps. The largest of the entertainment venues in Dalston was the North London Colosseum, located on the corner of Dalston Lane and Roseberry Place. It was built as a permanent circus (complete with stabling for animals) on the former rear gardens of 4–14 Dalston Lane, and could seat 3000 people. In 1897–8 the building was converted to a theatre; the circus ring was removed and a proscenium arch and fly tower

installed, and the building became Dalston Theatre. Between 1919 and 1921 the theatre in its turn was converted to a 'super-cinema', the Dalston Picture House. The interior was lavishly decorated with classical Greek motifs, and a tea room was installed on the first floor (Westman 2009, 32).

The cinema closed in 1960, the seats were removed, and for a time the stalls functioned as a car auction room. In 1965 the Four Aces nightclub opened in the building, eventually expanding into the tea room and rear stalls (Westman 2009, 33). The club was run by a young Jamaican, Newton Dunbar, who modelled it on the Apollo Theater, the music venue in Harlem, New York City, famous since the 1930s for launching the careers of many African-American musicians. The performers at the club represented the changing musical fashions of the day, including reggae from Desmond Decker and the Israelites, and funk and soul from Stevie Wonder. Among the famous who visited the club were Bob Marley, Norman Beaton, Mick Jagger, Jerry Hall and Chrissie Hynde. During a world tour in 1978 Bob Dylan looked in, on the same night as Sid Vicious and Nancy Spungeon (Burrows 2009, 144; Westman 2009, 35).

Nos 570–572 Kingsland Road

Neuberg and Company's Cinematograph Theatre, also named the Kingsland Imperial Picture Theatre, opened in December 1911 with seats for 500 people. The 3rd edition Ordnance Survey map is the earliest to show this establishment at 538–540 Kingsland Road (later renumbered as 570–572 Kingsland Road).

The cinema was in part owned by a Baroness von Neuberg, a German citizen; in November 1914, at the beginning of the First World War, von Neuberg's nationality and status as an enemy alien was given as a reason by the London County Council (LCC) for not renewing the cinematograph or music licences; the cinematograph licence was later renewed in March 1915. The building was constructed of yellow London stock brick laid in English bond; it had a flat reinforced concrete roof, supported by riveted steel plate girders carried on rectangular brick columns projecting from the internal face of the wall. The exterior of the cinema in Kingsland Road had a symmetrical facade of concrete, or faced with stone, and to either side of the entrance were pavilions of smooth banded rusticated stone with segmental pediments (Fig 127). Internally, the cinema auditorium was a large space, open to the ceiling, which was decorated with panels of sculpted papier-mâché on hessian.

Early in 1933 the cinema closed for refurbishment, re-opening in August of that year under its new name of the Plaza. A new stage, proscenium and screen were installed, along with illuminated signage and scrolled designs picked out in neon on the main elevation in Kingsland Road. Architect's plans of the building (LMA, GLC/AR/DS/06/312) show that the cinema comprised a large double-height auditorium, with seats raking down towards a stage and screen at the eastern end of the building. The cinema could seat 630 in the auditorium and 158

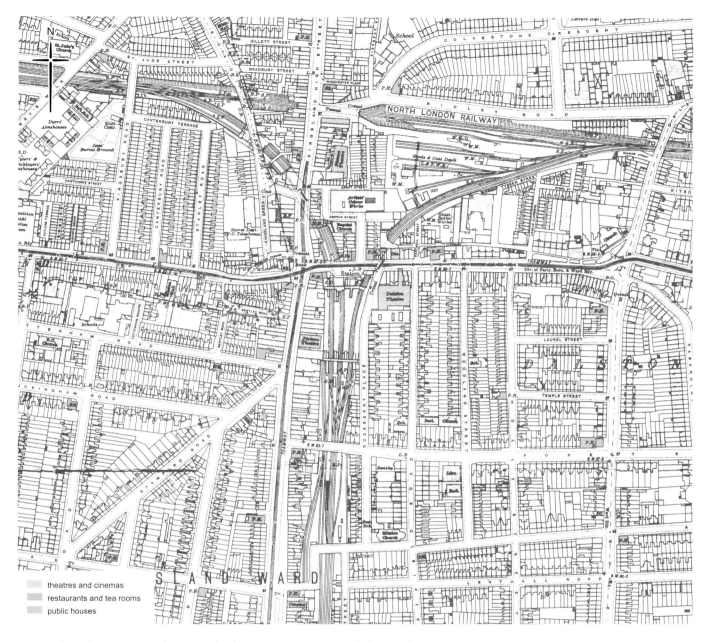

Fig 126 Places of entertainment in the vicinity of Dalston Junction station in 1916 (scale 1:4750)

in the balcony, which also accommodated the projectionist's booth. The basement, on the western side of the building abutting Kingsland Road, contained the staff facilities, storage and electricity generators.

Owing to the disruption caused by a road-widening scheme, the expiry of the entertainment lease, and loss of revenue due to the growing popularity of television, the Plaza cinema closed in December 1959, by which time it was owned by Kingsland Pictures Ltd. By 1962 the facade had been removed along with the projectionist's room, which had been located directly above the entrance to the cinema, and a reinforced concrete floor was inserted to create a separate first floor. The first floor was reached via a staircase from a separate street entrance in the south-western corner of the building. Plans of proposed alterations from 1962 (LMA,

GLC/AR/DS/06/312) indicate that the first floor was to be subdivided, creating a lettable space at the western end of the building, while the eastern end would be used by Smart Western, a firm of outfitters who occupied the ground-floor shop, as an additional sales room complete with hairdressers' concession, and with a staircase in the north-eastern corner leading to the ground floor.

The neon signage was removed from the front of the building, and the first floor became Chez Don, a nightclub which played host to the likes of the Rolling Stones, who performed there in November 1963. The building was later converted to a shop, the last occupant being Oxfam (Fig 128), who continued Dalston's live music tradition by hosting a series of concerts by artists including Jarvis Cocker and Fatboy Slim in the building.

Fig 127 The exterior of the Plaza cinema, Kingsland Road, Dalston, shortly after its closure in December 1959, looking north-east (HAD, HAP8214, image courtesy of London Borough of Hackney Archives)

Fig 128 The exterior of 570–572 Kingsland Road in 2007, looking east

6.6   Dalston after the Second World War

Parts of Dalston were subjected to heavy bombing during the Second World War (Fig 129). Infrastructure such as railway lines was a particular target, and to the south of Dalston the area around Lee Street and Haggerston Road, adjacent to the North London Railway line, was almost completely destroyed, as was Woodland Street to the south of Roseberry Place. Many of the terraces to the east of the railway line, and parts of the De Beauvoir Estate, were demolished and new social housing was built in their place.

The clearance of housing thought to be inadequate for life in the 20th century had begun before the Second World War, when in 1937 Frederick Place in Haggerston (Fig 130; Fig 131), a narrow lane adjacent to the eastern side of the Kingsland viaduct, was cleared of its 'slum' housing (*VCH* 1995, 28–33).

Passenger numbers on the railway line declined steeply after the Second World War as private ownership of cars increased. The station at Haggerston had closed after being damaged by bombing during the war, and never re-opened. Broad Street goods station was damaged by fire in 1951 and closed in 1969. Eventually the decision was made to close the railway line from Dalston to Broad Street, and the terminus itself. The demolition of Broad Street station began in the summer of 1985, and the station closed completely in June 1986. The decline of the NLR was rapid, and the closure of the station and removal of a direct rail link with the economic powerhouse of the City of London during the economic boom of the late 1980s further limited the post-war regeneration of the area. The relatively low cost of buying and renting housing, and industrial and retail premises in

Dalston during the second half of the 20th century has led to the lively and ethnically diverse character of the present neighbourhood. Like much of the East End, Dalston was settled by eastern European Jewish immigrants at the turn of the 20th century, and as the community grew more affluent and moved away, it was replaced in the 1950s and 1960s by a large Caribbean community, and in recent years by Turkish and Vietnamese émigrés, as well as by artists and designers looking for cheap studios and workspaces. Throughout the 20th century, Dalston maintained its reputation as a centre for entertainment, cemented by the announcement (by *The Guardian* newspaper, at least) that it was 'the coolest place in Britain' (Flynn 2009).

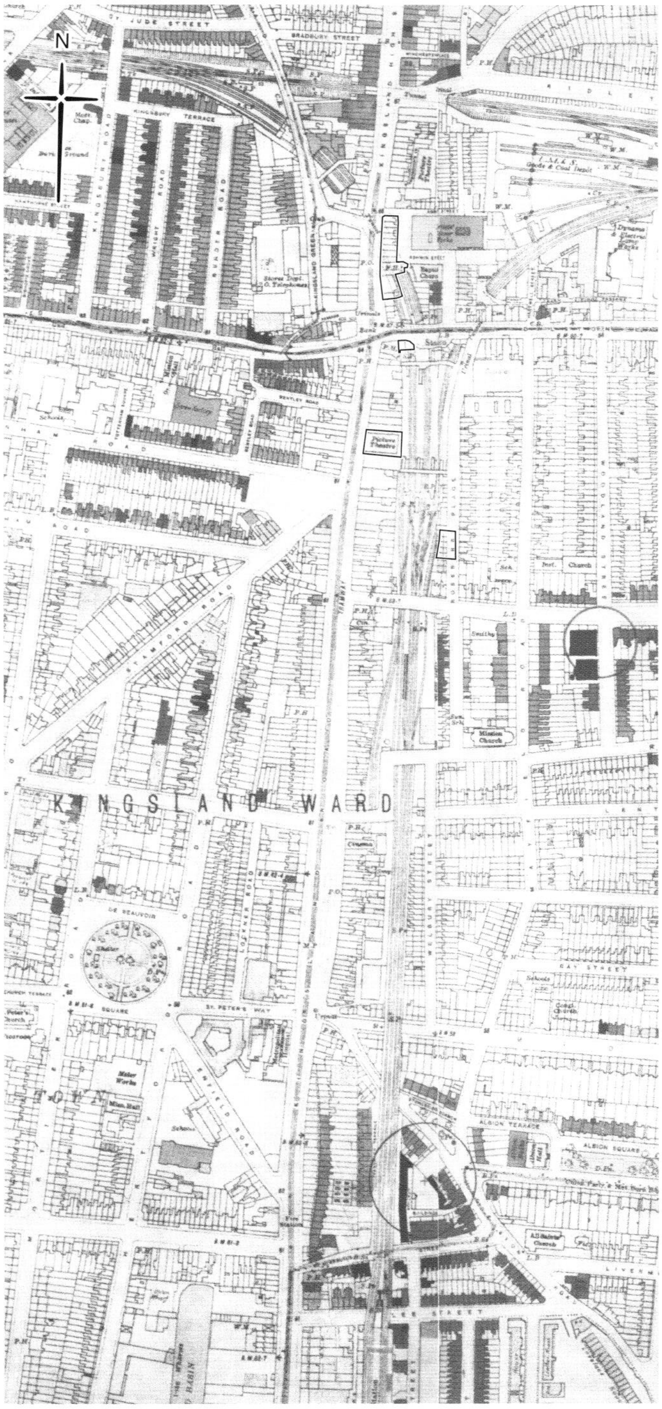

Fig 130 Frederick Place, Haggerston, prior to clearance in 1937, looking south (HAD, HAP2721, image courtesy of London Borough of Hackney Archives)

Fig 129 London bomb damage map, 1939–45, showing Dalston (Saunders 2005, map no. 40) (scale 1:4500)

Fig 131 An architect's model of the Frederick Place clearance area (HAD, HAP2722, image courtesy of London Borough of Hackney Archives)

7

Conclusions and future research

7.1   Railways and the East End

The extension of the East London line gave an opportunity to examine standing buildings and below-ground archaeology dating to the periods before, during, and after the construction of the Eastern Counties Railway, the North London Railway and East London line of the London Underground. The mid to late 19th century was a time of immense upheaval across the United Kingdom, when the building blocks of civic pride and commercial enterprise were laid, shaping the towns and cities we live in today. The railways facilitated urban sprawl and altered the way the metropolis was used; Dalston, along with many other former villages, became popular, bustling suburbs and attractive places to live for commuters to the City.

The changing technologies of the 19th century were manifested in the fabric of buildings, including railway stations, bridges and viaducts, and the construction of railway lines and viaducts shaped and changed the surrounding environment. Railway infrastructure both limited and facilitated movement, dividing streets and communities just as easily as it split them apart, by blocking off streets and creating physical and visual barriers. Yet the railway infrastructure itself provided opportunities, particularly the viaducts of the NLR and the GER, becoming cheap or free spaces for legitimate businesses, war-time shelter and criminality.

Archaeologists are increasingly looking at the 20th century from an archaeological point of view, recognising that the historic environment actively structures contemporary life, for example the street art and homelessness of Grimsby Street, and the live music scene of Dalston. However, archaeology requires a greater understanding of why buildings and structures take the form that they do, incorporating insights from engineering and the study of materials and technology, in order to achieve a better appreciation of how buildings and technology shape behaviour, and vice versa.

Beyond the railway infrastructure recorded here, the abandonment of the various backyard features and the objects used in their filling can be linked to the compulsory purchases and demolition of parts of Shoreditch High Street, Patience Street, King Street and St John Street by the ECR, and of Lee Street by the NLR, and provide useful snapshots for those wanting to study the range of material culture used in these East End streets. Clearly questions have to be raised about whether the objects left behind were gathered up prior to demolition or represent a final act of abandonment by the inhabitants themselves. However, the range of local makers represented by the clay pipes provides evidence that at least some of the rubbish was of local origin, and many groups, in particular those from King Street (Chapter 3.6), St John Street (Chapter 3.7) and Lee Street (Chapter 6.3) provide particularly rich and discrete assemblages suggestive of a household clearing episode. The similarly dated glass, crockery and clay pipes found here are all good examples of the sorts of 'proper dry rubbish' preferred for filling holes in the ground during the Victorian period (Jeffries 2006, 275). Although the interpretation of these groups could not be as progressive as that applied to the silk manufacturers of Spitalfields (Holder and Jeffries in prep) located to the west, and the transient maritime community of Regent Street in Limehouse to the east (Owens et al in prep), they add to the increasing body of data about individual East End households. Weaving together the life-cycles of people, place and things, and projecting this against the evictions and process of abandonment that took place in advance of railway construction, provides a useful mechanism by which the groups considered in this text can be interpreted further.

The greater complexity and quantity of standing structures, artefacts and documentary sources for the post-medieval period, and especially for the 19th and 20th centuries, combined with folk and living memory, may require some re-writing of the rules for how archaeology is done, and who should do it. The impact of the construction of the new railway on the neighbouring communities in Hackney has been successfully explored by an oral history recording and community collecting project undertaken by the London Transport Museum, and which formed the core of an exhibition, *Overground uncovered: life on the line*, held at the Museum between May 2010 and March 2011. This project, and others like it, offers the opportunity to compare responses to urban change, in both the past and the present.

Archaeological studies of the built environment have traditionally focused on buildings being 'read' and understood as they were intended to be by those responsible for their construction; however, 'the questions to be asked of any structure must involve the people who built, inhabited and abandoned or demolished it, and the wider situations in which it existed' (Hicks and Horning 2006, 282). Buildings have what Dan Hicks and Audrey Horning have termed 'afterlives' (ibid, 290), the persistence, change and decay that are the unintended elements of a life history. These messy biographies need to be acknowledged, and an increasing number of studies which take into account the multiple lives and interpretations of the built environment are now emerging. The distinctive contribution of a historical archaeology of buildings lies in working on material remains that have outlasted any 'original' intentions or meanings: the fragmented remnants of interactions between humans and materials.

The acknowledgement that buildings and places have their own biographies, which extend beyond what was originally intended, can be seen from the experimental architectural artwork entitled *Intact*, by the Office for Subversive Architecture (OSA). The OSA addresses issues relating to urban regeneration by provoking debate and creating awareness of the built environment, and the opportunities it presents for sensitive architectural development which addresses the needs of locals, as well as the need for proper treatment of urban space. *Intact*, an intervention based around the 'sludge house' of the water-softening plant adjacent to the Braithwaite viaduct in Pedley Street, has been introduced in Chapter 4.7, but Juliet Davis highlights the potential that the project, and others like it, has had for re-imagining the site while interacting with interpretations of the past (Davis 2008, 13, 22). The OSA

were keen that the transformation of the sludge house into something resembling a doll's house, or a suburban semi, should not be seen as a memorial, but instead as marking a moment in the life of the structure that was far removed from its intended use. Rather than creating a new building, they were adding a new architectural layer to the site and, in the process, a new page to its messy biography.

7.2   Re-imagining railways

An example of a structure with a similarly 'messy biography' is provided by the High Line, the viaduct of the New York Central Railroad track, constructed between 1929 and 1934, which for 50 years conveyed goods to the warehouses on the industrial waterfront of Manhattan's West Side. The High Line was designed to go through the centre of blocks, rather than directly over 10th Avenue, to avoid creating the negative conditions associated with the elevated subways. The artists' impressions of ornamental structures elevated above the bustling streets, which formed part of the subway company prospectuses of the late 19th century, were not believed; those living near the elevated subways feared the physical and economic shadow of the railway, and witnessed the beginning of what became a long-running (and to 21st-century ears, familiar) debate on whether the elevated subway would 'raise property values by improving access or reduce them through the negative externalities of noise, pollution and strangers' (Dennis 2008, 339).

The fate of the structure, which by the 1980s was redundant for its intended purpose, was taken up by the Friends of the High Line, who wished to turn it into a mid-air park. The administration of Rudolph Giuliani, mayor of New York City between 1994 and 2001, was 'hostile to the project – the Mayor's men apparently viewing it as exactly the kind of touchy-feely, hey, kids, let's make that broken-down railroad into a park! Upper West Side quixotism that would leave the whole city carpeted with moss if left unchecked' (Gopnik 2009, 48). This particular railway structure, like those encountered during the East London line project, held a much greater importance for the local community than just being an abandoned railroad: 'the High Line is just a structure, it's just metal in the air, but it becomes a site for everybody's fantasies and projections' (Robert Hammond, cited in ibid, 51).

The *Intact* project carried out by the OSA demonstrated the potential for re-imagining the structures within the built environment 'in a way that both preserves their spatial qualities and radically revises possibilities for their present use and meaning' (Davis 2008, 22), not only in a practical way, led by architectural practice and with implications for the future form of the built environment, but also as a way of understanding the biography of the historic built environment and its capacity to tell a variety of different stories relative to use, experience and memory. This can be linked with the formal and informal occupations, uses and reuses of the buildings and structures recorded during this survey, including the arches of the Braithwaite viaduct and Bishopsgate goods station.

The undertaking of this recording project has presented an opportunity to engage with the complete history of districts of east London, an area of continuing change:

> Through adaptive re-use [urban-vernacular architecture] … remains present, in fragile and heterogeneous form, on Brick Lane [and] Kingsland Road, richly faceted and increasingly rare shopping 'high streets' with thriving markets, in architectural environments that have roots in the 18th century, with later elements randomly intermixed. These places have been havens of urban vitality, where long-term poverty and the absence of planned improvement have left the 'conformable' notably absent. Heavily, casually and continuously rebuilt, altered and converted, they have been, and have depended on being, in healthy states of flux – contingent and vivacious, with immense and genuine cultural diversity. (Guillery 2004, 302)

GLOSSARY

Abutment: a solid **pier** or wall from which a bridge **span** begins

Broad gauge: usually applied to the 7ft 1/4in track **gauge** used by Isambard Kingdom Brunel on the Great Western Railway, the term refers to a line with a track gauge greater than the **standard gauge**

Covered way: a railway line at surface level, or in a **cutting**, which has been built over

Counterfort: an interior buttress, used to strengthen a revetment wall

Cut-and-cover: a method of constructing an underground railway line by excavating a deep channel, lining with masonry, and then roofing over

Cutting: where a channel has been excavated through higher ground to accommodate a railway line; in urban areas, like east London, these are lined with vertical retaining walls to eliminate the need for space-wasting sloped sides

Decking: the timber, iron or steel flooring of a **girder** bridge

Embankment: a linear earthwork constructed to carry a railway line over a valley or low-lying ground

Gauge: the distance between two rails

Girder: in the context of railway architecture, the horizontal structural members of a bridge

Jack-arch: a series of small arches, usually constructed of brick, springing from cast iron beams to form a bridge **span**, or the roof of a tunnel or **covered way**

Lattice girder: a composite **girder** where the upper and lower chords, or horizontal girders, are connected by criss-crossed diagonal members

Navvy: the general term for a railway construction worker, derived from the 'navigators' who built canals

Overbridge: a bridge carrying a railway, road or canal over another railway

Pier: the intermediate support for the arches or **girders** of a bridge with more than one **span**, or of a **viaduct**

Plate girder: a **girder** consisting of several iron or steel plates riveted or welded together

Pratt truss: a type of trussed **lattice girder** with alternating vertical and diagonal members between the upper and lower chords, or horizontal **girders**

Refuge: a recess in the lining wall of a tunnel or **covered way** in which railway workers can safely shelter when trains pass

Siding: a length of track separate from the operating railway where trains and rolling stock are accommodated when being stored or loaded

Span: the gaps between the **piers** and **abutments** of a bridge or **viaduct**

Standard gauge: the normal track **gauge** of 4ft 8 1/2in

Underbridge: a bridge carrying a railway over a canal, road or another railway

Viaduct: a long **underbridge** comprising a series of arches, carrying a railway over a wide valley or through a built-up urban area

FRENCH AND GERMAN SUMMARIES

Résumé

Elisabeth Lorans

L'amélioration et l'extension de la ligne East London du métro londonien comme élément de « London Overground » ont fourni l'occasion d'examiner les modes de vie du centre de la cité et des faubourgs entre le XIXe et le XXIe siècle ainsi que l'impact de la construction et du développement des chemins de fer sur la vie des londoniens. Le programme extensif de relevé du patrimoine bâti mené à bien, de Dalston dans le nord jusqu'à Surrey Quays dans le sud, est présenté dans ce volume, en étant intégré aux données de fouille des sites de la gare de marchandises de Bishopsgate et de Lee Street à Haggerston, ce qui éclaire les conditions de vie dans ces secteurs avant l'arrivée du chemin de fer et les forts changements subis alors par les habitants de l'East End.

Le réseau d'Eastern Counties Railway, inauguré en 1840, était l'un des plus précoces de Londres et contrairement à ses concurrents de même date, le Great Western Railway et le London and Birmingham Railway, il dut tailler à travers les rues denses et les industries de l'East End ; les résultats des fouilles de la gare de marchandises de Bishopsgate renseignent sur les modes de vie des secteurs urbains de Shoreditch et Spitalfields immédiatement avant et pendant la construction du chemin de fer. Est ainsi examiné le rôle des chemins de fer et des structures associées - qui représentaient des bâtiments d'un type entièrement nouveau au milieu du XIXe siècle - dans le façonnage des modes de vie des habitants de l'East End et dans leur manière de se déplacer dans la ville et de considérer leurs voisins.

Bien que l'Eastern Counties Railway ait fait partie de la première vague des sociétés de chemin de fer couvrant le pays, transportant marchandises et passagers sur de longues distances et suscitant de fortes réactions admiratives de la part des auteurs de récits de voyages, l'excitation fut de courte durée. Vingt ans plus tard, la construction des réseaux locaux, comme le North London Railway et l'East London Railway, établirent des liens entre les diverses communautés et industries de centres urbains tels que Londres, facilitant leur extension et permettant la création de métropoles. La compagnie d'East London Railway était fondée sur le Tunnel de la Tamise, conçu et construit par Sir Marc Brunel avec l'aide de son fils Isambard Kingdom Brunel. Le tunnel avait pour fonction de relier les habitants et les industries des deux côtés de la Tamise mais il fut un échec économique. Sa construction commença en 1825 et se poursuivit de manière intermittente pendant dix-huit ans. La compagnie d'East London Railway le racheta et le transforma pour l'incorporer à sa nouvelle ligne, qui devint plus tard la ligne East London du métro londonien. A partir des années 1860, le North London Railway transforma le village périphérique de Dalston en un secteur très actif de la ville, rempli de bars, de cinémas et de restaurants, qui étaient contrecarrés par les divertissements sans alcool offerts par exemple par le salon de thé Tee-To-Tum dans Kingsland High Street.

Les études archéologiques de bâti mettent en général l'accent sur une lecture et une compréhension des édifices tels qu'ils ont été pensés par leurs constructeurs. Cette publication quant à elle cherche à aller au-delà de l'interprétation des fonctions premières de ces bâtiments et structures afin de prendre également en compte leurs multiples usages et le devenir du bâti ancien.

Zusammenfassung

Manuela Struck

Verbesserung und Ausbau der East London Bahnlinie der Londoner U-Bahn als Teil der „London Overground" boten die Möglichkeit, das Londoner Leben in Innenstadt und vorstädtischen Bezirken zwischen dem 19. und 21. Jh. sowie die Auswirkungen von Bau und Entwicklung der Eisenbahn auf das Leben der städtischen Bewohner zu untersuchen. Ein ausgedehntes Bauaufnahmeprogramm stehender Strukturen und Gebäude wurde durchgeführt zwischen Dalston im Norden und Surrey Quays im Süden, dessen Ergebnisse zusammen mit denen der Ausgrabungen am Standort des ehemaligen Bishopsgate-Güterbahnhofs und von Lee Street in Haggerston Gegenstand dieses Bandes sind. So wird das Leben in diesen Stadtvierteln vor der Ankunft der Eisenbahn und die daraus resultierenden Tumulte der Einwohner des Londoner Ostens („East End") erhellt.

Die Eastern Counties Railway, die 1840 eröffnet wurde, war eine der frühesten Bahnlinien in London und schnitt – anders als die gleichzeitigen Great Western Railway und die London and Birmingham Railway – bevölkerte Straßen und Industrieanlagen des Londoner Ostens; die Ergebnisse der Ausgrabungen vom Bishopsgate-Güterbahnhof vermitteln einen Einblick in das Leben in den Innerstadtbezirken von Shoreditch und Spitalfields unmittelbar vor und während dem Eisenbahnbau. Es wird erörtert, welche Rolle die Eisenbahnen und die mit ihnen in Zusammenhang stehenden Anlagen, die in der Mitte des 19. Jhs. völlig neue Bautypen darstellten, im Leben der Bewohner des Londoner Ostens spielten, und zwar wie sie sich von einem zum anderen Ort bewegten und wie sich ihre Beziehungen zu ihren Nachbarn änderten.

Obwohl die Eastern Counties Railway noch Teil einer ersten Welle von Eisenbahngründungen in England war, die das Land überspannten, Güter und Menschen über lange Strecken transportierten und zu atemlosen und ehrfürchtigen Berichten über Bahnreisen von Reiseschriftstellern inspirierten, erfreute sich die Begeisterung nur kurzer Dauer. Zwanzig Jahre später verband der Bau der örtlichen Eisenbahnen wie die North London Railway und die East London Railway die verschiedenartigen Gemeinden und Industriegebiete städtischer Zentren wie London und ermöglichte dadurch die unkontrollierte Ausdehung städtischer Randgebiete und Entstehung der Londoner Metropole. Die East London Railway besaß ihre Wurzeln im Themsetunnel, der von Sir Marc Brunel unter Mithilfe seines Sohnes Isambard Kingdom Brunel entworfen und erbaut wurde. Der Tunnel sollte Gemeinden und Industriegebiete zu beiden Seiten der Themse verbinden und war ein wirtschaftlicher Reinfall; die Konstruktion des Tunnels begann 1825 und setzte sich in Abständen für 18 Jahre fort. Die East London Railway-Gesellschaft kaufte den Tunnel und baute ihn um, so dass er Teil ihrer neuen Bahnlinie wurde, die später die East London Linie der Londoner U-Bahn bildete. Seit den 1860er Jahren verwandelte die North London Railway Dalston von einem abgelegenen Dorf in einen blühenden Innenstadtbezirk, der voll von Kneipen, Kinos und Restaurants war, der die alkoholfreie Unterhaltung, angeboten etwa durch die Tee-To-Tum Teestube in Kingsland High Street, entgegentrat.

Die archäologischen Untersuchungen einer Baulandschaft konzentrieren sich traditionell auf die Gebäude, indem sie so „gelesen" und verstanden werden, wie sie von den für ihre Erbauung verantwortlichen konzipiert waren. Diese Publikation versucht über das Verständnis und die Interpretation der geplanten Nutzungen hinauszugehen, indem unter Berücksichtigung der „unordentlichen" Biographien und mehrphasigen Leben von Bauten um uns herum sowohl die geplanten Nutzungen als auch das Nachleben der historischen Baulandschaft betrachtet werden.

BIBLIOGRAPHY

Manuscript sources

Essex Records Office (ERO)

D/P 134/28/1 deposited bill and plan of the Eastern Counties Railway from Shoreditch to Yarmouth, scale 4in to 1 mile, 1835

D/Z 346/3460/49 water-softening plant, horse infirmary yard, Bishopsgate (Spitalfields), site plan showing proposed alterations (drawing no. C.1130), scale 1in to 16ft, 1934

Q/RUm 2/46 Eastern Counties Railway: Shoreditch station enlargement plan and book of reference, 1845

Guildhall Library (GL)

MS 6008A/7 Land Tax assessments: Christchurch, Spitalfields, 1847

MS 11936/541, no. 1184866 Sun Fire Insurance records, 1834

MS 11936/552, no. 1236023 Sun Fire Insurance records, 1836

Hackney Archives Department (HAD)

HAP2721 photograph: Frederick Place, Haggerston Road, Nos 4–17, looking north, c 1930

HAP2722 photograph: the architect's model of the Frederick Place clearance area, looking north-east

HAP7432 photograph: the North London Railway crossing the Kingsland Road, looking north towards Hoxton and Dalston, 1961

HAP8214 photograph: the Plaza cinema, Kingsland Road, Dalston, shortly after its closure in December 1959

London Post Office trade and street directories, 55th to 117th editions (1854–1916)

M698 Anon, An account of the parish of St Leonard Shoreditch, c 1873

M3560 particulars of sale of lands no longer required by the North London Railway

M7612 deeds for property in Bryant Street, 1839–41

V2 Mr Lee's estate plans, 1790

Hulton Archive, a division of Getty Images

2665050 photograph: the German Gotha GVb bomber

Imperial War Museum (IWM)

ART 935 painting: *The Underworld: taking cover in a Tube station during a London air raid*, by Walter Bayes, 1918

London Metropolitan Archives (LMA)

DC/ED/009 map of the estate of Mr Lee, Esq, 1775

GLC/AR/DS/06/312 Imperial Cinema, Fish and Kebab House, Plaza Cinema, 538–540 Kingsland Road, Hackney LB: Building Act case file (Cinemas, Restaurants and Shops)

LCC/PP/BR/088 London County Council, alterations to

bridges for tramways, 27 April 1904

MJ/SP/1834/03 Court Sessions papers for March 1834

MJ/SP/1834/07 Court Sessions papers for July 1834

MR/PLT 5717–52 Land Tax assessments: St Leonard Shoreditch, 1811–32

SC/PHL/01/361 photograph: the railway arch and tenements of Reliance Square, Shoreditch, in 1898

SC/PHL/02/626 photograph: the main entrance to Bishopsgate goods station in 1962

SC/PHL/02/627 74/13851 photograph: Bishopsgate railway terminus in 1862

SC/PHL/02/629 photograph: the southern side of Bishopsgate goods station in 1955

London Metropolitan University East End Archive: the Paul Trevor Collection

B-120-17 photograph: the Sunday market in Brick Lane, 1976

B-137-09 photograph: gathering for a demonstration in Brick Lane, organised by the Bengali Youth Movement Against Racism, June 1978

London Transport Museum (LTM)

1983/4/361 poster: *The East London Railway restored*, by Charles Sharland, 1913

1990/76 poster: *We've turned the East London line orange to aid you*, by an unknown artist, 1990

1998/43369 East London Railway poster, with text in Yiddish

1998/48134 photograph: station gardens competition, 1945; three of the judges, accompanied by woman porter Mrs Metherall, inspecting her garden at Shoreditch underground station

1998/48904 photograph: severe air-raid damage to the exterior of Wapping underground station, October 1940

1998/56043 photograph: Wapping station in 1934

1998/65115 photograph: booking hall, Shoreditch underground station, East London line

Museum of London (MOL)

LIB5788 painting: *Over London by rail*, by Gustave Doré, 1872

National Railway Museum (NRM)

SX1114 photograph: a railwayman standing outside the Great Eastern Railway's horse infirmary at the Pedley Street viaduct, *c* 1911

SX1821 photograph: the Spitalfields water-softening plant, 1937

SX1822 photograph: the interior of the Spitalfields sludge house, 1937

NLR, Laurie Ward collection, box 2, album 9, 1925/6 photograph: the former Dalston Kingsland railway station in the early 20th century

The Old Bailey (OB)

t18340515-81 *Henry Edwards was indicted for that he, on the 23rd of April, at St Matthew, 1 piece of false and counterfeit coin, resembling, apparently intended to resemble and pass for, a current silver coin, called a shilling, feloniously did falsely make and counterfeit, against the Statute*, 15 May 1834

t18430227-892 *George Tappin was indicted for feloniously receiving of an evil-disposed person, on the 11th of Feb., 4 oz. weight of silk, value 10s.; and 9 wooden bobbins, 3d.; the goods of Charles Harris*, 27 February 1843

t18991211-77 *Louisa Josephine Jemima Masset (36) was indicted for, and charged on the Coroner's Inquisition with, the willful murder of Manfred Louis Masset*, 11 December 1899

Parliamentary Archives (PA)

HL/PO/PB/3/plan 1846/E41 Eastern Counties Railway: Shoreditch station enlargement plan and book of reference, 1846

The National Archives (TNA): Public Record Office (PRO)

CAB/23/5 minutes of a meeting of the War Cabinet, held at 10 Downing Street, SW1, on Tuesday, January 29, 1918, at 11.30am

HO 107/694/7, fos 26–38 census returns for the parish of Bethnal Green (part), township 3, 1841

HO 107/710/1, fos 5v–8 census returns for the parish of Christchurch Spitalfields, 1841

HO 107/1543, fos 228v–229 census returns for the parish of Christchurch Spitalfields, 1851

RAIL 186/2 minutes of the Provisional Committee of the Eastern Counties Railway, 22 October 1835

RAIL 186/92 Eastern Counties Railway: accounts for contracting work at Bishopsgate and Mile End, 1847–8

RAIL 1008/34 letters to the Secretary of the Great Western Railway, 1842–53

RG 10/505, fo 5 census returns for the parish of Christchurch Spitalfields, 1871

Tower Hamlets Local Studies Library (TH)

LH82/70/30 photograph: the railway bridge over Brick Lane, *c* 1976

Printed and other secondary works

Addley, E, 2006 The story of a wall, *The Guardian*, 30 September www.guardian.co.uk/artanddesign/2006/sep/30/art.streetart

Agricola, G, 1556 *De re metallica*, Basel

Allen, C J, 1975 *The Great Eastern Railway*, Shepperton

Allen, R, 1998 *The moving pageant: a literary sourcebook on London street-life, 1700–1914*, London

Anon, 1823 Mr Hawkins' plan for a tunnel under the Thames, *Mechanic's Mag*, 6 December, 225–6

Anon, 1847 *A guide to the Eastern Counties and Norfolk Railway*, London

Anon, 1881 The Great Eastern's new goods depot, *Engineering* 1881, 221

Anon, 1918 Aliens in air raids, *The Times*, 2 February, 3

Anon, 1964 Big depot fire cuts railway services: two men die, *The Times*, 7 December, 6

Ayris, I M, Nolan, J, and Durkin, A, 1998 The archaeological excavation of wooden waggonway remains at Lambton D pit, Sunderland, *Ind Archaeol Rev* 20, 2–22

Beaudry, M C, 2006 *Findings: the material culture of needlework and sewing*, New Haven and London

Beeton, I, 1870 *Beeton's book of needlework*, London

Best, C, 2003 Reading graffiti in the Caribbean context, *J Popular Culture* 36, 828–53

Betts, I, 2009 Assessment of the ceramic building material from Bishopsgate goods station, London E1 (BGX05), unpub MOL rep

Birchenough, A, Dwyer, E, Elsden, N, and Lewis, H, 2009 *Tracks through time: archaeology and history from the London Overground East London line*, London

Birchenough, A, Bull, R, Davis, S, Lewis, H, and Wroe-Brown, R, in prep *Holywell Priory and the development of Shoreditch before 1600: archaeology from the London Overground East London line*, MOLA Monogr Ser

Bird, J (ed), 1922 *Survey of London: Vol 8, Shoreditch*, London

Blackmore, L, 2009 Assessment of the pottery from Grimsby Street, London E2 (GIM07), unpub MOL rep

Blackmore, L, and Egan, G, 2009 Assessment of the glass from Lee Street, London E8 (LSD05), unpub MOL rep

Booth, C, 1889 *Descriptive map of London poverty*, reproduced in Hyde, R, and Reeder, D, *Charles Booth's 'Descriptive Map of London Poverty', 1889*, 1984, London

Bourne, G, 1920 *William Smith, potter and farmer, 1790–1858*, London

Brighton, S A, 2001 Prices that suit the times: shopping for ceramics at The Five Points, *Hist Archaeol* 35(3), 16–30

Brooks, A, 2005 *An archaeological guide to British ceramics in Australia 1788–1901*, Sydney

Bull, M, 2007 *Banksy locations and tours: a collection of graffiti locations and photographs in London*, London

Burrows, T, 2009 *From CBGB to the Roundhouse: music venues through the years*, London

Carrow, J M, and Oliver, L, 1846 *Cases relating to railways and canals, argued and adjudged in the Courts of Law and Equity, 1842 to 1846, Vol III*, London

Cattell, J, and Falconer, K, 2000 *Swindon: the legacy of a railway town*, Swindon

Charlton, L E O, 1936 *War over England*, London

Cherry, B, and Pevsner, N, 1998 *The buildings of England: London 4, North*, London

Clapham, J H, 1916 The Spitalfields Acts, 1773–1824, *Econ J* 26, 459–71

Connor, J E, 2000 *The Great Eastern light: a history of the Great Eastern Railway's electric light generating station at 233 Shoreditch High Street, London*, London

Coysh, A W, and Henrywood, R K, 1982 *The dictionary of blue and white printed pottery 1780–1880*, Woodbridge

Davies, P, 2009 *Lost London 1870–1945*, Swindon

Davin, A, 1996 *Growing up poor: home, school and street in London 1870–1914*, London

Davis, H, 1991 *Chinoiserie: polychrome decoration on Staffordshire porcelain 1790–1850*, London

Davis, J, 2008 Re-imagining Bishopsgate goods yard, *Architect Res Q* 12(1), 12–25

Dennis, R, 2008 *Cities in modernity: representations and productions of metropolitan space 1840–1930*, Cambridge

Dickens, C, 1848 *Dombey and Son* (Penguin Classics edn, 2002), London

Doyle, R, and Leigh, P, 1849 *Manners and customs of ye Englyshe*, London

Dwyer, E, 2009 Underneath the arches: the afterlife of a railway viaduct, in Horning and Palmer 2009, 351–64

Egan, G, 2009 Assessment of the accessioned finds from Bishopsgate goods station, London E1 (BGX05), unpub MOL rep

Flynn, P, 2009 Welcome to Dalston, now the coolest place in Britain, *The Guardian*, 27 April www.guardian.co.uk/uk/2009/apr/27/dalston-cool-london-suburb

Francis, J, 1851 *A history of the English railway: its social relations and revelations 1820–45, Vol 2*, London

Gavin, H, 1847 *Unhealthiness of London and the necessity of remedial measures: being a lecture delivered at the Western and Eastern Literary and Scientific Institutions, Leicester Square and Hackney Road*, London

George, M D, 1925 *London life in the 18th century*, London

GER Soc website Great Eastern Railway Society website: www.gersociety.org.uk (last accessed March 2008)

Godden, G A, 1969 *Caughley and Worcester porcelains 1775–1800*, New York

Godden, G A, 2003 (1964) *Encyclopaedia of British pottery and porcelain marks*, London

Goodwin, J, and Barker, D, 2009 *Small pieces of history: archaeological ceramics from Tunstall, Stoke-on-Trent*, Stoke-on-Trent Archaeol Service Monogr 2, Stoke-on-Trent

Gopnik, A, 2009 A walk on the High Line: the allure of a derelict railroad track in spring, in Sternfeld, J, *Walking the High Line*, 47–52, Göttingen

Goslin, G, 2002 *John Braithwaite and the Bishopsgate viaduct*, London

Green, C, 1999 *John Dwight's Fulham pottery: excavations 1971–9*, London

Greenwood, C, and Greenwood, J, 1827 'Map of London from an Actual Survey', reproduced in Margary, H, 1982 '*Map of London from an Actual Survey' by C and J Greenwood, 1827*, Margary in assoc Guildhall Library, Kent

Grey, T, 2009a Assessment of the clay pipes from Bishopsgate goods station, London E1 (BGX05), unpub MOL rep

Grey, T, 2009b Assessment of the clay pipes from Grimsby Street, London E2 (GIM07), unpub MOL rep

Grey, T, 2009c Assessment of the clay pipes from Lee Street, London E8 (LSD05), unpub MOL rep

Guillery, P, 1995 Bishopsgate goods station, unpub RCHME rep

Guillery, P, 2004 *The small house in 18th-century London: a social and architectural history*, New Haven and London

Harvey, A D, 1992 *Collision of empires: Britain in three world wars 1793–1945*, Oxford

Hicks, D, and Horning, A, 2006 Historical archaeology and buildings, in *The Cambridge companion to historical archaeology* (eds D Hicks and M C Beaudry), 273–92, Cambridge

Higgins, D A, 2004 The clay tobacco pipes, in Keevill, G, *The Tower of London moat: archaeological excavations 1995–9*, Hist Roy Palaces Monogr 1, 241–70, Oxford

Holder, N, and Jeffries, N, with Daykin, A, Harward, C, and Thomas, C, in prep *Spitalfields: the history and archaeology of the London suburb 1539–1860*, MOLA Monogr Ser

Hook, J, 1995 *They come! They come!: air raids over London during the 1914–18 war: Vol 3, parts 4 and 5: The raids of 1918*, London

Horning, A, and Palmer, M (eds), 2009 *Crossing paths or sharing tracks?: future directions in the archaeological study of post-1550 Britain and Ireland*, Woodbridge

Horwood, R, 1813 Plan of the Cities of London and Westminster, the borough of Southwark, 3 edn, reproduced in Margary, H, 1985 *The A–Z of Regency London*, Margary in assoc Guildhall Library, Kent

Hudson, E W, 1896–7 Holywell Priory, Shoreditch, *J Roy Inst Brit Architects* 3 ser 5, 469–71

Hughes, R, 1979 Bridges and viaducts, in *Railway architecture* (eds M Binney and D Pearce), 140–59, London

Jackson, A A, 1985 *London's termini*, Newton Abbot

Jackson, P (ed), 1969 *John Tallis's London street views, 1838–40: together with the revised and enlarged views of 1847*, London Topogr Soc Pub 110, London

Jeffries, N, 2006 The Metropolis Local Management Act and the archaeology of sanitary reform in the London Borough of Lambeth 1856–86, *Post-Medieval Archaeol* 40(2), 272–90

Jeffries, N, Owens, A, Hicks, D, Featherby, R, and Wehner, K, 2009 Re-materialising metropolitan histories?: people, places and things in modern London, in Horning and Palmer 2009, 323–50

Johnson, J, 1823 A plan to erect an iron tunnel under the Thames, *Mechanic's Mag*, 20 December, 257–61

Kay, P, 1999 Railway archaeology sites: Brick Lane, *London Railway Rec*, January, 156–63

Keith, M, 2005 *After the cosmopolitan?: multicultural cities and the future of racism*, Abingdon

Kellett, J R, 1969 *The impact of railways on Victorian cities*, London

Kershen, A J, 2005 *Strangers, aliens and Asians: Huguenots, Jews and Bangladeshis in Spitalfields 1660–2000*, London

Knight, C, 1841 *London, Vols 1–2*, London

Knight, C, 1851 *Knight's cyclopedia of London, no. 36: metropolitan railway stations*, London

Lee, C E, 1976 *The East London Line and the Thames Tunnel: a brief history*, Westminster

Letherby, G, and Reynolds, G, 2005 *Train tracks: work, play and politics on the railways*, Oxford

Lewis, S, 1849 *A topographical dictionary of England*, London

Lichtenstein, R, 2007 *On Brick Lane*, London

Litvinoff, E, 1972 *Journey through a small planet*, London

London Transport Museum, 2002 London Transport Museum station history: Shoreditch (extract from internal museum database)

Macdonald, N, 2001 *The graffiti subculture: youth, masculinity and identity in London and New York*, Basingstoke

Mander, D, 1996 *More light, more power: an illustrated history of Shoreditch*, London

Matthewson, A, Laval, D, Elton, J, Kentley, E, and Hulse, R, 2006 *The Brunels' tunnel*, London

Miller, G L, Samford, P, Schlasko, E, and Madsen, A, 2000 Telling time for archaeologists, *Northeast Hist Archaeol* 29, 1–22

Miller, T, 1852 *Picturesque sketches of London*, London

Morgan, B, 1965 The Bishopsgate goods depot fire, *Modern Railways*, February, 80

Morgan, K, 2001 *The Oxford history of Britain*, Oxford

Morrison, A, 1896 *A child of the Jago*, London

Morriss, R, 2003 *The archaeology of railways*, Stroud

Nabarro, R, and Richards, D, 1980 *Wasteland*, London

OSA website Office for Subversive Architecture website: www.osa-online.net/de/flavours/up/intact/a/index.htm

Oswald, A, 1975 *Clay pipes for the archaeologist*, BAR Brit Ser 14, Oxford

Owens, A, Jeffries, N, Featherby, R, and Wehner, K, in prep Fragments of a modern city: material culture and the rhythms of everyday life in Victorian London, *J Victorian Culture*

Pearce, J, 2009 Assessment of the pottery from Bishopsgate goods station, London E1 (BGX05), unpub MOL rep

Pearce, J, Bull, R, and Davis, S, in prep Industrial development and suburban growth in London during the 17th and 18th centuries, *Trans London Middlesex Archaeol Soc*

Penrose, S, and Trickett, P, 2004 Peds versus Pods: conflict and the M32, a paper presented at the Contemporary and Historical Archaeology in Theory conference, University of Leicester, 19 November 2004

Pfautz, H W, 1967 *Charles Booth on the city: physical pattern and social structure*, Chicago

Phillpotts, C, 2009 Holywell Priory, London EC2, and Bishopsgate goods yard, London E1: documentary research report, unpub MOL rep

Poole, B, 1852 The economy of railways as a means of transit, comprising the classification of the traffic, in relation to the most appropriate speeds for the conveyance of passengers and merchandise, *Proc Inst Civil Engineers* 11, 450–9

Reynolds, G W M, 1845 *The mysteries of London*, London

Richards, J, and MacKenzie, J M, 1986 *The railway station: a social history*, Oxford

Richardson, B, 2009 Assessment of the accessioned finds from Grimsby Street, London E2 (GIM07), unpub MOL rep

Rischin, M (ed), 1987 *The Jews of North America: proceedings of a conference sponsored by the Multicultural History Society of Ontario, held at the University of Toronto, April 24–26, 1983*, Detroit

Robbins, M, 1967 *The North London Railway*, 6 edn, London

Roberts, C, 2005 *Cross river traffic: a history of London's bridges*, London

Robson, W, 1830 *Robson's London directory*, London

Robson, W, 1835 *Robson's London directory*, London

Rocque, J, 1746 'A Plan of the Cities of London Westminster and Southwark with contiguous buildings from an actual survey' by John Rocque, reproduced in Margary, H, 1971 *'A Plan of the Cities of London Westminster and Southwark' by John Rocque, 1746*, Margary in assoc Guildhall Library, Kent

Rothstein, N K A, 1987 Huguenots in the English silk industry in the 18th century, in Scouloudi 1987, 125–40

Samuel, R, 1973 Comers and goers, in *The Victorian city: images and realities* (eds H J Dyos and M Wolff), 123–60, London

Samuel, R, 1981 *East End underworld: chapters in the life of Arthur Harding*, London

Saunders, A (ed), 2005 *The London County Council bomb damage maps (1939–45)*, London

Savage, G, and Newman, H, 2000 (1974) *An illustrated dictionary of ceramics*, London

Scouloudi, I (ed), 1987 *Huguenots in Britain and their French background, 1550–1800: contributions to the historical conference of the Huguenot Society of London, 24–25 September 1985*, Basingstoke

Select Committee of the House of Commons, 1847 *Railway labourers and labourers on public works: report of the Select Committee of the House of Commons appointed to inquire into the condition of the labourers employed in the construction of railways and other public works*, London.

Shaw, D, 1914 *London in the sixties, by 'one of the Old Brigade'*, London

Sheppard, F H W, 1957 *The Survey of London: Vol 27, Spitalfields and Mile End New Town*, London

Simmons, J, 1995 *The Victorian railway*, London

Smith, J, and Rogers, R, 2006 *Behind the veneer: the south Shoreditch furniture trade and its buildings*, Swindon

Stanford, E, 1862 'Stanford's Library Map of London', reproduced in Margary, H, 1980 *'Stanford's Library Map of London' 1862*, Margary in assoc Guildhall Library, Kent

Starling, T, 1831 *Map of the parish of Hackney*, London

Subterranea Brit website Subterranea Britannica website: www.subbrit.org.uk

Sussman, L, 1997 *Mocha, banded, cat's eye, and other factory-made slipware*, Stud Northeast Hist Archaeol 1, Boston, Mass

Timbs, J, 1868 *Wonderful inventions: from the mariner's compass to the electric telegraph*, London

Troske, L, 1892 *Die Londoner Untergrundbahnen*, Berlin

VCH, 1966 *The Victoria History of the county of Essex: Vol 5* (ed W R Powell), London

VCH, 1995 *The Victoria History of the county of Middlesex: Vol 10* (ed T F T Baker), London

VCH, 1998 *The Victoria History of the county of Middlesex: Vol 11* (ed T F T Baker), London

Watson, B, 2004 *Old London Bridge lost and found*, London

Weightman, G, and Humphries, S, 1983 *The making of modern London 1815–1914*, London

Weinstein, R, 1984 Pipeclay figurines, in Thompson, A, Grew, F, and Schofield, J, Excavations at Aldgate, 1974, *Post-Medieval Archaeol* 18, 122–4

Westman, A, 2009 Dalston Theatre and adjacent buildings, 4–14 Dalston Lane, Roseberry Place and Beechwood Road, London E8: a standing building survey report, unpub MOL rep

Wise, S, 2008 *The blackest streets: the life and death of a Victorian slum*, London

White, J, 2003 *Rothschild Buildings: life in an East End tenement block 1887–1920*, London

Whiter, L, 1978 (1970) *Spode*, 2 edn, London

Whitting, P D (ed), 1965 *History of Hammersmith*, London

Wolmar, C, 2005 *The subterranean railway: how the London underground was built and how it changed the city forever*, London

Wolmar, C, 2007 *Fire and steam: a new history of the railways in Britain*, London

INDEX

Compiled by Margaret Binns

Page numbers in **bold** indicate illustrations and maps
All street names and locations are in London unless specified otherwise
County names within parentheses refer to historic counties